D1602562

DEMOCRACY IN EUROPE

DEMOCRACY IN EUROPE

Legitimising Politics in a Non-State Polity

Heidrun Abromeit

Berghahn Books
New York • Oxford

First published in 1998 by

Berghahn Books

© 1998 Heidrun Abromeit

Library of Congress Cataloging-in-Publication Data
Abromeit, Heidrun.
    Democracy in Europe : legitimising politics in a non-state
polity / Heidrun Abromeit.
        p.   cm.
    Includes bibliographical references and index.
    ISBN 1-57181-985-1 (alk. paper).
        1. Democracy--European Union countries.
        2. Political participation--European Union countries.
        3. Legitimacy of governments--European Union countries.
        4. Referendum--European Union countries.
        I. Title.
    JN40.A27   1998
320.8'094--dc21   98-24534
                                                        CIP

British Library Cataloguing in Publication Data
A catalogue record for this book is available from the British
Library.

TABLE OF CONTENTS

Contents

FOREWORD

This book serves a double purpose: It submits a practical proposal for the democratisation of the European Union; and by doing so the book is meant to contribute to the current academic debate on how to make democracy fit to survive in an age of globalisation. It is not difficult to detect 'democratic deficits' in the modern world in general and in the European Union in particular; but it is apparently very difficult to find remedies for them. For some time now a frustrated public has been looking on in a kind of stupor at how political integration in Europe seems to be going all awry, while baffled academics have in vain been rummaging in the tool box of (parliamentary) democratic theory, seeking instruments fit to tackle the obvious political dilemmas. Up to now only a few authors have gone any further than to state the necessity of a new 'transformation' of democracy; fewer still have set about devising new models of a (possibly) 'post-parliamentary' democracy.

This book undertakes to do just that. It contends that the answer to the riddle of European democracy is not the basically statist one of constitutionalisation-cum-parliamentarisation, but the more flexible one of supplementing the European decision-making process with various direct-democratic instruments. Such a model of post-parliamentary democracy (or so the author hopes) should be of interest to political practitioners as well as to political theorists. Attempting not to bore the political audience by taking too long to come to the point, I have tried to unfold my argument as briefly as possible – a procedure which I hope will not alienate an academic audience who might have preferred a more detailed discussion of the theoretical aspects.

This book (as all others) would not have been completed without the help, comments, criticism and support of the author's friends and colleagues. Hence I duly thank all of them. In particular, my thanks are to Anna Geis, Natalie Fryde and Anne Schneidau-Lappi who did their best to 'de-Germanise' my English; to

Kirsten Mensch and Thomas Schmidt who eagerly discussed the pros and cons of my proposal; to Ruth Zimmerling, Rainer Schmalz-Bruns and all other colleagues who pointed out my errors but whose advice I did not always heed; to Hans Hirter and Michael Nentwich who gave information on specific issues; to Karlheinz Reif who gave support in Brussels and to all those European Community officials who patiently answered my questions and showed an interest in my project; to Tanja Hitzel-Cassagnes who finally streamlined the manuscript; and last but not least to Moritz who suffered most but never tired of cheering me up.

Darmstadt, March 1998.

H. Abromeit

LIST OF ABBREVIATIONS

BDA	Bundesvereinigung der Dutschen Arbeitgeberverbände
BDI	Bundesverband der Deutschen Industrie
BVerfG	Bundesverfassungsgericht
BVerfGE	Bundesverfassungsgericht Entscheidungen
CoR	Committee of the Regions
CSU	Christlich-Soziale Union
EC	European Community
ECG	European Constitutional Group
ECJ	European Court of Justice
EMU	European Monetary Union
EP	European Parliament
EPP	European People's Party
ESC	Economic and Social Committee
ESK	Europäische Strukturkommission
ESP	European Socialist Party
EU	European Union
FRG	Federal Republic of Germany
GDP	Gross Domestic Product
GG	Grundgesetz
GMO	Genetically-Modified Organism
IGC	Intergovernmental Conference
MEP	Member of the European Parliament
MP	Member of Parliament
NGO	Non-Governmental Organisation
PMI	Philip Morris Institute
QMV	Qualified Majority Voting
SEA	Single European Act
TEC	Treaty of the European Community
TEU	Treaty of the European Union
UNICE	Union des Confédérations de l'Industrie et des Employeurs d'Europe
VAT	Value Added Tax

1

INTRODUCTION

What Kind of Animal is the European Union?

Ever since the European Community came into being, students of
political science and of international relations as well as those of
international and of constitutional law (less though, surprisingly,
the 'informed public') have been wondering what kind of animal
it is – and what it is going to become, once the integration process
has come to an end. For the EC Treaty of 1957 envisages a steady
and dynamic progress towards the completion of a European
unified or 'Single Market'. As the European Court of Justice (ECJ)
made clear at an early stage this *telos* and such progress are to take
definite precedence over all other considerations; hence the treaty
(as interpreted by the Court) has set in motion a continuous drive
to increase the powers of the community. Yet while the treaty left
no doubt as to the goal of *economic* integration, it was mute about
the latter's *political* implications which since then have kept
political analysts busy.

In the beginning, the political practice of European integration
took the shape of intergovernmental cooperation. To this day the
member-state governments take their pride in remaining the
'masters of the treaty' – after 'Maastricht I' perhaps even more
than in the years before. From the start, however, the community
had institutions of its own, namely the Commission and the ECJ as
the main agents intended to keep the integration process in
motion. As a consequence, the national governments may still be
'masters of the treaty', that means those who determine the EC's
primary law which consists of the treaties and possesses a quasi-
constitutional quality; but they are not the only source of its
secondary law which consists of 'regulations' and 'directives' (i.e.,
its quasi-normal legislation), rounded off by European Court

rulings. And what is more: while the primary law requires ratification by the national parliaments, the secondary law nowadays mostly does not; it is binding law in all member states without any further ratification.

Both the juridical side of the matter and the 'state-like' institutions of the Commission, European Parliament (EP) and ECJ have caused what may be called the 'statist analogy': the longer it exists, the more the EC resembles a normal state. In fact (as Weiler argues, 1996, p. 517ff.) it has achieved a sort of 'constitutional order' marked by the elements of 'Supremacy' (of EC law), 'Direct Effect' (of EC law on member-state citizens) and the judicial *Kompetenz-Kompetenz* which the ECJ allots to itself. Yet its state-like quality seemed for a long time to be restricted to the (admittedly wide) field of economics. In most other areas even intergovernmental cooperation has remained scant. Put in the words of the ECJ (in the Van Gend & Loos case of 1962) 'the Community constitutes a new legal order ... albeit within limited fields'. It would be too simple, however, to define the EC as a state-like structure with jurisdictional competence in a comparatively narrow range of issues. The treaty's inherent teleology prevented a neat and orderly division of competences between the nation-states and the community. The latter is, in actual fact, neither truly restricted to one or few policy area(s) nor has it blanket coverage. Instead in an apparently unsystematic fashion it covers 'bits and pieces', more or less great chunks of various policy areas.[1] The logic hidden behind the resulting muddle (if there is one) is that of 'implied powers' accruing in the process of establishing a Single Market or, in 'Euro-speak', simply that of the 'effet utile'.

In recent years the Single European Act and the Maastricht Treaty have added new dimensions to the muddle. (1) There are issues and political questions which can be decided by a majority (in the Council of Ministers), while others require unanimity. (2) Depending upon the type of decision, more or fewer actors – and more or less institutionalised ones – participate. (3) In a 'Europe of variable geometries' (due to opt-outs and the 'Europe of different speeds'), varying sets of member states take part in 'common' policies or in arrangements for mutual coordination. To complete the picture of the muddle which is currently prevailing, one may add that actual decision-making is increasingly occurring in informal policy networks rather than in the formal institutions –

1 See the list given in Marks et al. 1996, p. 125f.

not least because of the uneven and asynchronous allocation of policy making powers just mentioned.

From this sketchy diagnosis we may conclude (1) that the EC (or, now, EU) is not the kind of *confederation* of states one has got accustomed to in history which leaves members both free to enter and exit as they please and free to organise and enact policies at home as they like. The EU binds members too closely together – and to the community itself – and restricts their internal autonomy too much to be called a confederation. At the same time it is too flexible in its range of coordinated policies as well as in the allocation of competences to resemble the typical *confederatio*. (2) Nor can the EU for similar reasons be classified as an international *'policy regime'*: members are bound too closely and over too wide a range of policy issues; its regulating powers are not restricted to firmly specified policy areas. In this respect one might at best call it a disjunct *number* of 'regimes'. (3) Above all, the EU is no *federation* – not least because it is not and does not want to be a state (although Euro-sceptics feel that it increasingly looks like one). In other words, we are dealing with a polity that is 'horizontal, polycentred, infranational' (Weiler 1996, p. 519) on the one hand but that has managed to constitute firm hierarchies of norms, in various fields, on the other.

To put a name to this strange sort of polity and to allow classification, other types of associations have been introduced into the debate as, for instance, the *'Nationalitätenstaat'* or multinational state based on the model of the Austrian-Hungarian 'Doppel-monarchie' of former times, which granted a relatively high degree of internal autonomy to 'nationalities' (Lepsius 1991); the *consortio* based on the model of the association of firms cooperating 'in the performance of functional tasks that are variable, dispersed and overlapping' (Schmitter 1996, p. 136); the *condominio* 'based on variation in both territorial and functional constituencies' (ibid.). As far as I can make out, this latter variant is the only one to combine the two distinct dimensions of European policy making: the territorial (regional) and the functional (sectoral) one. While it seems to have become quite a fashion to characterise the EU as a *'dynamic multi-level political system'* (Jachtenfuchs & Kohler-Koch 1996), emphasising the three-level structure of community, member states and subnational units, the sectoral dimension as it is embodied in the informal policy networks is rarely taken into consideration.

Even more widely spread – and longstanding – is the mode of depicting the EC/EU as an entity or polity *'sui generis'*, which is of little use either for classification or for clarification. The same can be said of a new trend to refer to 'postmodernism' and throw into the wind all the above-named analogies as relics of bygone modernity. In fact the whole debate and the quest for the adequate categorisation might be viewed as a mere *l'art pour l'art*, were it not for two necessities: (1) to be quite clear about the non-state character of the European polity, and (2) to find a clue to the structure of European policy making (in case there is one that is stable) which describes it as accurately as possible.

The Legitimatory Gap

Both necessities are equally important when it comes to the question of *legitimate* political decision-making. Obviously European decisions result in law and in regulations which bind the member states and affect their citizens directly. Ever since the war-cry 'no taxation without representation' the core idea of modern democracy has been that no one shall be forced to do (or pay for) things he would not do of his own free will without his having had a say in the matter, either directly or via representatives; any alternative must be considered 'illegitimate'. The core of every representative system is its parliament. Hence the widespread conviction is that 'the main challenge for the EU is the current impossibility of creating a true parliamentary basis for democracy' (Andersen & Eliassen 1996, p. 3). There is, of course, an institution called the European Parliament. But it is neither a true legislative body: only since Maastricht does it possess certain powers of 'co-decision' with the Council, which means that in effect it has a modicum of blocking power. Nor is it a body to enforce 'political responsibility', that is, to hold a government responsible to its electorate. Reasons for this may be manifold and in due course I shall come back to them in greater detail; but at the bottom of them all lie the two basic facts that the EU is no 'normal', i.e., state-like, polity and that there is no European electorate in the proper sense.

While direct parliamentary legitimacy is lacking, it used to be argued that community policy making could rely on the indirect legitimacy provided by the national parliaments holding the 'masters of the treaty', the member-state governments, responsible at home. For at least two reasons this indirect link has proved rather fragile and dubious almost from the start: (1) Council decisions are usually more or less precarious compromises based on complicated package-deals. Governing majorities in national parliaments are put under some pressure not to wilfully destroy those precious achievements of negotiative art; to withhold their consent would be a downright snub to their own government. (2) As has already been mentioned, the EC's secondary law does not require ratification by member-state parliaments. Furthermore, a steady process of 'creeping' expansion of community powers has taken place which was never put to the test of ratification because it was set in motion and driven forward by Court rulings lying beyond the reach of parliamentary control. (3) If indirect legitimacy is to be more than merely formal the national electorates ought to be given the opportunity, in national elections, to express an opinion on European issues, a prerequisite which is clearly lacking in reality. (4) Since the Single European Act of 1986 prescribed (qualified) majority voting for a number of Council decisions the indirect legitimisation has become even more threadbare: in those countries whose governments had been outvoted in the Council the latter's decision would be flatly illegitimate.

Not much seems to be gained then by way of indirect legitimisation. As parliamentary – or democratic – legitimisation can neither directly nor indirectly be won some Euro-politicians and a number of political scientists have looked around for other ways in which European policy making might be rendered legitimate. They believe they have found the solution in something called 'functional legitimacy'.[2] The problem with this notion is that it is rather imprecise. In principle it could mean two things: (1) It could refer to a specific kind of participation or representation along the lines of sectoral ('functional') groups instead of territories. Thus corporatist systems could be said to be functionally legitimised. (2) It could refer to the performance of the system, again defined along functional lines. Thus a system solving problems efficiently could be said to be functionally legitimised. Authors have not always been very clear about which of the two notions they prefer; sometimes they even muddle them. This is the case, for example, when reference to the 'functional effectiveness' of community policy making is coupled with that to the participation of many and different actors in it (Wessels 1996, pp. 559, 63). In reality, however, in quite a number of issues it is just the 'functional effectiveness' which is in doubt. And what is

---

2   See, for instance, Wolfgang Wessels, in: Andersen & Eliassen 1996, p. 59ff.

also dubious is the way in which the actions of those manifold European actors are linked to the interests of citizens, group members, etc. In both respects the Common Agricultural Policy may serve as a vivid example of a policy which has produced discontent instead of functional legitimacy. The fact that the EC is nonetheless attractive to political and business élites of countries outside (ibid., p.64) can hardly make up for such shortcomings which are somewhat bitterly registered inside the Union.

So we are left with a definite legitimatory gap which is nowadays mostly called 'democratic deficit'. This did not make itself very much felt in the days of the 'permissive consensus'; however, these days are gone.[3] According to the Eurobarometer all possible indicators for support of the EU on the part of the citizens in its member countries have been going down consistently since early 1991.

This very statistical fact seems to have taken European and national politicians by surprise. While the political science debate in the last decade at least had been full of references to and remedies for the 'democratic deficit' of the EC, politicians had been blind to the decline in acceptance which became abundantly clear when the ratification of the Maastricht Treaty threatened to get stuck in those countries where a referendum was a legal prerequisite. With the laudable aim of making amends for the former neglect of public opinion, in the run-up to the 1996 Intergovernmental Conference a 'Reflection Group' was installed with the explicit task of finding ways of reducing the deplorable gap between the community and the ordinary citizen. The Group's proposals were rather modest (see Reflection Group 1995). Few of them were of an institutional kind; what is more, those proposals which were concrete enough to be put into practice were qualified and substantially modified in the following sentence, thus mirroring the lack of consensus between member states about the further development of the EU. Apparently, in the matter of making the Union more democratic and bringing it closer to its wider populace agreement could only be reached upon two items: that of making European politics more 'transparent' (which means issuing more information and includes such impressive demands as that to render the treaty itself more readable), and that of simplifying its decision-making procedures.

Meanwhile the political debate has again moved miles away from the issue of improving the EU's institutions and procedures,

---

3 For the early 'permissive consensus' see Inglehart 1971; for its further development see the Eurobarometer surveys, as well as Noelle-Neumann 1992; Reif 1993.

leave alone the issue of remedying its democratic deficit. Lately the all-encompassing question has been the economic one of how to achieve monetary union in the teeth of sluggish economic performance, high and growing unemployment as well as high and growing public sector deficits nearly everywhere. Put more precisely, the question was how the 'convergence criteria' agreed upon in Maastricht can be met by how many members in what time, and whether the requirement of the states' new borrowings not exceeding 3 per cent of the GDP should mean 3.0 or 'three point something'. The debate upon the Euro and the size of the 'core Europe' has cast into the shadow all other issues, including the fairly fundamental one of whether one wants a 'wider' or a 'deeper' Union. The Intergovernmental Conference has tried hard to stick both to the agenda and to the timetable envisaged for 'Maastricht II' but Chancellor Kohl hinted at the end of the Dublin summit (of 4-6 October 1996) that a 'Maastricht III' might be necessary to deal with the institutional and constitutional problems. Yet there are doubts whether they will ever be dealt with at all.

The Aim of this Book

In a situation such as this a book dealing with just these latter problems might look a trifle out of place. The dwindling acceptance by the Union's member peoples, however, cannot be 'trifled with' much longer, especially since the Union is unavoidably becoming ever more 'political'. At least since 'Maastricht I' the EU has been saddled with a constitutional problem[4] which cannot be solved by ignoring it. On the contrary, the problem will not only make itself increasingly felt in Brussels but is bound to have repercussions in member states, causing severe legitimatory problems at that level too. The constitutional issue is the more pungent because of the elusive and complex nature of the polity which is to be 'constitutionalised', and which is threatening to grow into an ogre, in the eyes of beholders, if it is not restrained. There seems to be but one other alternative, that is, to turn back the clock and return to 'stage one', to the initial common market. There are observers (as

---

4   Weiler (1996, p. 518) gives a specific interpretation of this problem: 'The condition of Europe ... is not, as is often implied, that of constitutionalism without a constitution, but of a constitution without constitutionalism. What Europe needs ... is not a constitution but an ethos and a *telos* to justify ... the constitutional order it has already embraced.' This view, however, may appear a trifle over-modest.

well as Euro-sceptic politicians) who believe that this is exactly what will – and should – happen, particularly in the case of further enlargement of the community. But whoever thinks that the EU has passed the 'point of no return' (see Schmitter 1996, p. 122) will have to look very hard for both adequate and practicable solutions for its constitutional problems.

The aim of this book is to do just this: to devise ways and mechanisms of legitimising and democratising a political system that is characterised by (1) various levels (community – member states – subnational units) as well as (2) various dimensions (territorial and 'functional') of policy making; that combines (3) highly complex formal (institutionalised) as well as (4) equally complex informal ways of decision-making; that binds together, furthermore, (5) actors of various degrees of 'europeanisation', acting (6) in policy areas of different degrees of europeanisation and (7) with different numbers of participants, agreeing policies (8) under different decision-making rules. And perhaps this long list of complexities is not even complete. A further point to be kept in mind is the Union's (actual as well as deliberate) non-state character which from the outset precludes a whole range of constitutional devices as both inadequate (disregarding the enormous complexity of the European puzzle) and impracticable (disregarding the professed intentions of the 'masters of the treaty'). To sum up: the task of this book is to find an answer to the question of how to democratise the European Union without 'federalising' it. That is, this book will not tackle all the EU's major problems but only deal with one (albeit a decisive one) of them. A second limitation should be made clear from the start: it will be primarily a theoretical exercise, exploring various political theories and trying to deduce elements of a model for the democratisation of a complex, multi-dimensional polity from them.

Yet before it comes to that, I shall briefly discuss a second deficit of the EU, one that is closely related to the legitimatory one: its lack of openness in the sense of being compatible with the member states' different political systems and their governing constitutional principles (chapter 2). I shall proceed to review the main reform proposals for the EU's future development which have been discussed in public in recent years and which mostly seem to be inadequate solutions to the constitutional problem (chapter 3). In its major part (chapter 4) the book will then consider the possible theoretical foundations of a model of multi-level and multi-dimensional democracy. The theories to be examined are: (1) contract theory which may give valuable hints at alternative ways of democratising political systems – or, more precisely, at alternatives to parliamentarisation; (2) the theory of fiscal federalism which federalists as well as their opponents use to consult when it comes to the 'proper' way of allocating decision-making powers between territorial units; (3) theories of group representation which may help to find out ways of how to deal with the sectoral (functional) dimension of European politics; (4) game theory and network analysis which I hope are of some use in clarifying the (mostly hidden) structure of decision-making in policy networks and hence in depicting possible 'intervention points' for democratic control. (5) Finally, new concepts of democratic theory such as those of 'reflexive' or 'associative' democracy have made tentative proposals to open up ossified political structures and to democratise complex societies. I shall examine them and try to establish their practical value.

As a result of this exercise, a model based on the use of direct-democratic minority rights and combining the territorial and the sectoral bases of politics will be proposed and submitted for further discussion. Its elements are: (1) a direct-democratic veto of those regions which possess autonomous status and feel materially threatened in that autonomy by European integration or certain European policies; (2) an optional referendum granting a similar veto right to 'functional groups', or more precisely, to the assumed reference groups of European issue networks (including those who suffer from their policies); (3) a mandatory referendum to legitimise any new contracts or quasi-constitutional steps. These instruments will be explained in some detail as well as illustrated by some (fictitious) examples in chapter 5, and the most probable objections to be brought forward against them argued with in chapter 6. The impatient reader who is interested in practical political proposals rather than in the theories on which they are founded may be advised to proceed directly to chapter 5.

However convincing my proposal might be, the chances that it will be avidly seized and applied by politicians are unfortunately remote. This is why the concluding chapter will have to come back to current political developments in Europe. It will contrast constitutional necessities with the interests and strategies of the actors in the European arena and deduce from this a prognosis about the likeliest course of events – and about the consequences these developments will have, at supranational and national levels, for democratic legitimacy.

2

INCOMPATIBILITIES

The EU considers itself by no means complete – neither institutionally nor politically (i.e., concerning the policy areas it covers) nor as regards membership. The new EU treaty's *telos* is the 'ever closer union of the peoples of Europe' (Art. 4 Maastricht Treaty), aiming, rather explicitly, at complete coverage of major policies, at laws equally binding all over the community, at efficient 'governance'. One might suppose it aims at the real 'super-state'. More implicit is the other *telos* hinted at with the vague notion of '*the* peoples of Europe': that of uniting all European countries. Both goals are contradictory, however: the more state-like and complete in one respect the Union grows, the more difficult it will become to integrate further members, i.e., to become complete in the other respect. This is what Euro-politicians mean when they argue that a choice may have to be made between 'deepening' or 'widening' the EU, i.e., between further institutionalisation and constitutionalisation and enlargement.

Yet the contradiction may exist only on the face of it. It may be possible to devise forms of association which allow for closeness between members and at the same time flexibility or 'tolerance' towards their different institutions, cultures, traditions, etc. It becomes ever more urgent to invent such 'tolerant' structures the more the Union intends to associate or integrate members which have developed various types of democratic government.

Most Euro-politicians and a number of observers would argue at this point that such tolerance is exactly what characterises the EU and that 'in practice, the Community's institutional framework has been sufficiently elastic to allow different concepts of political organisation and hierarchy to survive and coexist.' (Kirchner 1994, p. 256). Likewise, the Reflection Group comments upon the necessary 'flexibility' of the Union's common policies, albeit not of its institutions. At the same time, however, it states firmly that there is, and must be, a *limit* to flexibility (thus confirming, incidentally, the view already mentioned that in the process of integration the 'point of no return' has long been reached). The limits include, foremost, (1) the '*acquis communautaire*' which means that any progress made in integration is deemed irreversible, and (2) the consolidation of a 'unified institutional framework' as the safeguard of cohesion within the Union. It is exactly these two limits which render the EU of today incompatible with the various 'different concepts of political organisation' alluded to above and with various constitutional concepts. As a consequence, in future would-be members will see themselves confronted not only with a higher threshold before entry but also with fiercer domestic conflicts about it: membership will then be identified with the necessity to give up crucial elements of one's own identity. This is exactly the problem of the Swiss which will be considered later. Moreover, in becoming more rigidly institutionalised the EU will to the same extent devaluate crucial elements of the political systems of the old member countries, with the effect of, in the long run, delegitimising them. Today the European super-structure already generates incompatibilities which make themselves increasingly felt in member societies, probably causing more discontent than any legitimatory deficit at community level does.

The concept of 'sovereignty'

One problem of incompatibility is apparently unavoidable: the conflict of 'sovereignties'. The principle of 'supremacy' of European law is to be read in the way that the community has created 'a new legal order ... for the benefit of which the states have limited their sovereign rights';[1] and 'direct effect' means that the EC/EU is not 'an international organisation belonging to the States which created it' (Weiler 1996, p. 520) but a new polity with 'sovereign rights' of its own, making the citizens of member states its 'subjects'. The legal

1   ECJ: Van Gend & Loos v. Nederlandse Administratie der Belastingen; case 26/62 (1962), ECR 1; quoted in Weiler 1996, p. 521. See also Usher 1981 (p. 19ff.), who quotes the conclusion drawn by the British House of Lords Select Committee on the European Communities (in its 22nd Report, Session 1977/78) that the direct effects even of directives (!) cause 'an irreversible removal of legislative power from the United Kingdom Parliament' and thus imply 'a transfer of sovereignty' (p. 36f.).

construction, as may be concluded from this, is one of divided or 'dual sovereignty', known from federations and especially from American constitutional history. This is not the place to enter into the juridical debate about whether it is possible (or reasonable) to conceptualise sovereignty – i.e., the state's *plena potestas* – as divisible. Early theorists of sovereignty (such as Bodin, 1583) would flatly negate such a notion as a *contradictio in adjecto* since sovereignty is defined (*inter alia*) by its indivisibility, while Diceyan orthodoxy would argue that divided authority leaves no room for sovereignty but at best brings forth 'the predominance of the judiciary' (Dicey 1885/1959, p. 175). The point which is of interest here is that, depending on constitutional concepts and fundamental constitutional principles, the clash of sovereignties can pose more or less acrimonious problems for the political classes of member states.

The difference between Britain and Germany in this respect may serve to illustrate my point.[2] Britain's problems with EU supremacy are obvious, and one would misinterpret their acerbity if one laid them solely at the door of party politics. Since the days of the Tudors and the invention of the figure of the 'King in Parliament', the notion of 'parliamentary sovereignty' has been the core of British constitutionalism. In modern times it grew into the governing principle of British parliamentary democracy. It found its classical formulation in Dicey's dictum (ibid., p. 39f.) 'that Parliament ... has ... the right to make or unmake any law whatever; and, further, that no person or body is recognised by the law of England as having a right to override or set aside the legislation of Parliament.' No law, no written constitution, no court nor any other institution, not even the people of Britain, can normally (with rare exceptions) and rightfully limit the Parliament's *plena potestas* – but now European laws, courts and institutions do just this: 'override and set aside the legislation of Parliament'. In 1974 Lord Denning warned that 'the Treaty is like an incoming tide. It flows into the estuaries and up the rivers' (quoted in Mount 1992, p. 219); meanwhile many British feel they will be drowned in the flood. Even Mrs Thatcher tried to stem it in vain, under the battle-cry of the British people's right 'to govern themselves under their own laws' (quoted in Judge 1993, p. 190).

As a solution to the puzzle of how to profit from the economic advantages of a common market while avoiding the political and judicial implications of European integration, the British

2 For the following see Abromeit 1995.

government hit upon the ingenious strategy of 'opting out'. There could be no matter of overruling parliamentary decisions (or only a negligibly formal one) as long as the British government had given its consent to community regulations preceding British law; and where the government withheld its consent, Britain at the same time would 'opt out'. Yet, lacking the traditions of judicial review and constitutional courts, the British had not reckoned with the European Courts. The ECJ has in a number of cases since the 1980s 'overridden and set aside the legislation of Parliament'. Together with the European Court of Human Rights it has tried to impose some sort of written constitution (in the shape of the bill of human rights) on an unwilling political system. The worst of it is that the ECJ flatly disregards the cleverly devised 'opt-out' strategy. Although Britain opted out of the European Social Charter, the Court ruled in November 1996 that the British would have to comply with the community's directive limiting working hours (a directive not formally based on the Charter, but closely connected to it as regards content). This in fact is the plainest collapse of the doctrine of parliamentary sovereignty imaginable. The 'hysteria' which the British political class is accused of in regard to Europe ought to be seen in this dramatic light of a constitutional concept, clung to for centuries, fast dissolving.

While British Europhobia is at least partly owed to the conviction that European integration violates the core principle of British constitutionalism, the Germans' apparent ease with European supremacy can be explained by the absence of any notion of sovereignty in German constitutional thinking. In the tradition more of the *Rechtsstaat* than of democracy the core of German constitutionalism is the concept that every institution and every 'power' of the modern state is bound by the (written) constitution and, hence, not sovereign. Not even 'the people' is exempt from this principle: it is *pouvoir constitué* like all the others. German constitutional law abhors boundless power in any shape and therefore attempts to do without any notion of *pouvoir constituant*. Such abstinence results in an apparent paradox: the claim is that of 'constitutional patriotism' which considers the *Grundgesetz* (Basic Law) as sacrosanct; but the practice is one of frequent and easy amendments of the same *Grundgesetz* (GG). Of course, the cavalier treatment of the GG is facilitated by the fact that *Bundestag* and *Bundesrat* do not have to ask the people for their consent since there is no *pouvoir constituant*.

Considering the constitution sacrosanct and leaving no room for a sovereign is only one side of the coin of German constitutionalism. The other is that a watchdog to guarantee compliance with the constitution by all the constituted powers is needed: that is, a constitutional court. The *Bundesverfassungsgericht* obviously takes its role as a watchdog extremely seriously and exercises its competences expansively – so much so that according to some commentators it has by now filled the vacant post of sovereign (see Abromeit 1995, p. 60). Frequently taking the *Bundestag* majority to task over its legislation (i.e., 'setting aside' its decisions), it has grown into a kind of super-legislator, providing MPs with detailed guidelines about the proper ways to regulate (for instance) party finance, social policy, university structure or abortion law (see, especially, Landfried 1984). In doing so its rulings have more often than not been based less on the wording than on the 'spirit' of the written constitution, less on the actual articles than on their 'essence'. Since those rulings, once issued, are transformed into elements of the constitution themselves, the court is not only legislator but constituent power. Only recently it has just stopped short of ruling an amendment of the GG unconstitutional.[3] Interestingly enough, the better part of the German public would hardly have been surprised had the court done so. In fact, quite a number of commentators were left rather disappointed.

The point to be made in this context is that the political class in Germany has grown accustomed to the fact that parliamentary decisions are overruled. Used to a concept of legitimacy emphasising legality instead of decision-making by elected representatives, the precedence of European law and the effect of ECJ rulings do not give rise to more than momentary irritation since they do not touch upon fundamental principles. Additional constituted powers present few difficulties where all powers are *pouvoirs constitués*. Instead of clashes of sovereignties the new layer of politics only produces conflicts of competences – and those, in their turn, can (in principle) be solved by courts. In this view the gravest of possible problems then would be how to allocate competences between those, i.e., (in this case) between the German Constitutional Court and the ECJ.

The lesson to be learnt by this comparison is that constitutional systems which rely on judicial review and on constitutional courts can more easily be integrated into supranational polities than those

---

3   In the case of the amendment of Art. 16 GG, concerning the right to seek asylum in the FRG; 14.05.1996.

which are not. On the other hand, the specific way the European super-structure operates, in particular its own reliance on court rulings in the development of community powers, must necessarily estrange political systems characterised by definite concepts of sovereignty. Switzerland – not yet a member and with a public torn over the issue of joining – would be another case in point. Here the clash of sovereignties is exacerbated by the fact that the Swiss notion of 'popular sovereignty' is tightly bound to that of democracy.[4] It is with the people (that of Switzerland and/or that of the *Kantone*) that the final political decisions rest. To have them overruled by European courts would mean to undermine Swiss democracy; for many Swiss citizens it would literally amount to an end of self-government. This is why the question of whether or not to join the EU has grown into a question of Swiss identity as well as into a constitutional issue:[5] those favouring the entry frankly concede that the Swiss constitution is 'not Europe-fit' and suggest changing it into a 'Europe-compatible' one (Germann 1990, p. 26ff.).

Federalism

To an impartial observer, however, such a conclusion seems to tackle the problem from the wrong end. When constructing a super-structure like the EU, would it not have been much more sensible to take care from the start that the structure itself was compatible with the various potential members' constitutions, instead of expecting them to alter theirs to be 'Europe-compatible'? The disregard on the part of the European edifice for fundamental traits of members' political systems can be exemplified by a brief examination of how federations can survive within the Union. At the beginning only one member state (Germany) was a federation; now there are three of them. One of them (Belgium) as yet has little federalist practice while both Germany and Austria are not exactly what a 'sworn federalist' would call 'true' (or dual) federations, marked by a substantial autonomy of the *Länder*. A fourth federation – Switzerland – names the probable weakening of *Kanton* autonomy as one of the major reasons for resistance against joining.

Both historically and theoretically federalism can be seen as a device to integrate heterogeneous, regionally segmented societies.

---

4 For a short introduction to the political system of Switzerland see Linder 1994 (esp. p. 130ff.).
5 See Weibel & Feller 1992; Linder et al. 1996.

More precisely: Federalism is supposed to aggregate territorial units with distinct identities to form a common polity *without* being forced to give up those identities. Such aggregation/integration is achieved (1) by guaranteeing *separate* spheres of authority and jurisdiction to territorial units and the 'federal' level and (2) by guaranteeing that as a rule none of the subunits will be *outvoted* on issues touching on their specific identities. The first principle implies that there are two distinct levels of government and that legislative competences are divided between them unambiguously and in such a way that each of the two levels has the final say (i.e., 'sovereignty') in a number of matters. The second principle means that component units have the right of 'co-decision' (bordering on or extending to veto rights) at federal level. Generally speaking, federations would seem to be the ideal partners for supranational association since they are used to a practice of shared or 'divided sovereignty'. At the same time, one would think that the EU, composed of fairly heterogeneous territorial entities as it is, would necessarily possess traits of a federation itself and, hence, be structurally compatible with any federation amongst its members.

Unfortunately, the EC has long since acquired traits of the 'decentralised unitary state'. From the outset the EC treaty's inherent teleology mentioned above (and its enforcement by ECJ rulings) prevented the unambiguous allocation of competences to community and member-state levels. More specifically, neither the old nor the new treaty envisage a workable and enforceable mechanism for the allocation of powers which recognises the component units of federalist member states as separate jurisdictions. The principle of subsidiarity laid down in Art. 3b TEC (as inserted by Art. G (5) TEU) which is neither unambiguous nor enforceable anyway, applies (as most commentators agree) to the relationship between community and states only and not to that between community and subunits (or 'regions'). The Committee of the Regions added to the European institutions in 1992 (see below) is not entitled to have a say in the matter of competences. Had it existed from the start, it would not have been in a position to stem the flood of expanding community powers. Nor has the reform of the European Structural Funds in 1988 truly upgraded the regions. Although it prescribes a 'three-sided partnership of the Commission, member states, and regional authorities', the role the latter are allowed to play is defined by the national governments: 'To the extent that subnational units of governance exist in the Community, they do so at the behest of member states. They have no legal standing independent of the states of which they are a part.' (Marks 1992, pp. 211, 215).

Those two principal weaknesses – lack of division of competences and lack of legal recognition of subunits – have had, in practice, the two consequences (1) that European secondary law has increasingly infringed upon subunits' discretionary powers. Whatever safeguards may exist for the units' competences and autonomy 'at home', that is, do not provide guarantees at community level.[6] As regards the German *Länder*, the new community competences constituted by the Maastricht Treaty now threaten the last stronghold of *Länder*-autonomy, their '*Kulturhoheit*' (cultural autonomy).[7] (2) Yet the second consequence might hurt even more, for the subunits do not lose powers solely to the community. What makes matters worse is that the process of integration alters the *internal* balance of federations, i.e., strengthens the federal (or central) level *vis-à-vis* the regional one. Wherever regional interests are at stake in European politics it is the national governments' consent that is required, not that of regional authorities; no matter how much the latter may lobby the Commission they will have no voice in any decision. Thus their dependence on national governments acquires a new quality. When both practical consequences are combined, the effect European integration has so far had on the territorial dimension of politics may with good reason be called 'inverse regionalism' (Weiler 1995, p. 8).

Small wonder, then, that the German *Länder* have judged 'Europe' to be the greatest challenge since 1946 to the survival of German federalism and to their own political weight. Untypically for German constitutional tradition, the Basic Law provided no help in this plight, since in Art. 24 GG it states unequivocally that 'the federation' is entitled to transfer sovereign rights to supranational authorities, without any obligation to ask the *Länder's* consent. Yet the only way to make their voice heard in Europe at all is indirectly, i.e., via the federal government for the EU primary law ignores them. So the *Länder* busied themselves with some success to obtain a modicum of constitutionally 'safe'

6 That there may be subunits which would prefer their competences to be invaded by European rather than by their own federal authorities (as some Swiss *Kantons* apparently do), is another matter and due to long-standing rivalry between the two levels of government.
7 This particular sphere of autonomy can now be invaded in matters of broadcasting and of vocational training; others (so it is feared) will follow.

influence on that government's European policy. An amendment of the Basic Law in 1994 prescribes that in EU matters the *Länder* representation *Bundesrat* is to be heard and informed by the federal government; and whenever these matters have direct impact upon *Länder* competences, the *Bundesrat's* view is even to be 'considered as decisive'. That this procedure heightens the political importance of the *Bundesrat* but does not necessarily protect the single *Länder's* interests is another story, not to be laid at the door of European developments.

It may be interesting to note that the new Belgian federation at least constitutionally protects regional interests and autonomy better than the German one. In case of treaty revisions, all subnational parliaments will be asked for approval before the Belgian one can ratify them. This means that 'one obstinate subnational ... parliament ... can block' a European agreement entering into force (Kerremans 1997, p. 12). In reality, however, such an event is highly unlikely, the 'political threshold' being too high for it to happen. Furthermore, the Belgian 'political class', despite all language and other cleavages, seems fairly united in an overtly pro-European stance. Yet whatever the devices found in federal member states, European primary law being what it is, it will be rather difficult to safeguard regional interests and the subunits' autonomy in the European quasi-'super-federation'. Hence the Swiss federation is probably quite right to be so sceptical about joining it.

Democracy

Interestingly enough, the German Constitutional Court had nothing to say on federalist matters[8] when it was called to comment upon the EU Treaty's compatibility with the Basic Law in 1993.[9] It concentrated on problems of domestic democratic legitimacy instead. As a supranational association and *'Staatenverbund'*,[10] i.e., a non-state, so the Court argued, the EU lacks a democratic legitimation of its own which fulfills the standards set by the

---

8 This is not the Court's fault, but follows from the appeal it had to decide upon, which was mainly concerned with the citizens' rights from Art. 38 GG. There are other instances, however, where the Court ruled in a much more roundabout way.
9 BVerfGE 89, 1993, 155-213. For comments see Weiler 1995.
10 The BVerfG obviously wishes to indicate with this classification that the EU is something in between the *federatio* and the *confederatio*.

'principle of democracy' fixed in the German constitution. The civil rights bestowed upon German citizens in Art. 38 GG are therefore safeguarded only as long as democratic legitimacy within Germany remains intact – that is, as long as sufficient and sufficiently 'substantial' decision-making powers rest with the German *Bundestag*. In the case at hand the Court ruled that this stipulation was 'still' given, hence the Maastricht Treaty remained (just) compatible with German constitutional law. It did so although it itself had established that domestic democratic legitimation is in doubt the moment when EC treaty norms can – and will – be interpreted in a way that expands explicit community competences; or, in other words, when a sort of *Kompetenz-Kompetenz* is (more or less tacitly) accepted. The judges obviously took some trouble to convince themselves that there was no such danger, Art. F III Maastricht Treaty, Art. 109 j, Art. 235 or other relevant articles of the TEC notwithstanding, and that Germany remained one of the 'masters of the treaty' and as such a 'sovereign state'.

Commentators of the Court ruling as well as observers of European developments tend to take a different view, pinpointing the 'erosion of parliamentary democracy' and characterising the EU as 'an instance of post-parliamentary governance' on both community and member-state level (Andersen & Eliassen 1996, p. 227). Generally speaking, there may be two sides of 'post-parliamentarianism': (1) a shift of powers of decision-making and control from legislative bodies to the executive, and (2) a shift of powers from parliaments to non-parliamentary and non-governmental actors, such as neo-corporatist structures and policy networks. Both aspects of the phenomenon are not new but have for decades been recognised as traits of 'modern' governance.[11] The European polity and the effect its policy making has on parliamentary systems in member states appear, however, to mark a further turning of the screw, particularly where the balance between parliaments and governments is concerned. EU politics essentially is an arrangement of the executive – of national governments regarding formal decisions, of the administrators of lower (regional) and upper (European) levels as well as of business firms and interest groups if one includes the informal aspects of policy making. There are increasingly fewer occasions in this process where national parliaments are involved for there is increasingly less need to ratify European decisions at home.

---

11 See, for instance, Judge 1993; Lehmbruch & Schmitter 1982.

As we know EC legislation has either 'direct effect', i.e., is immediately in force in member states (regulations), or binds member-state parliaments as regards content, i.e., reduces their activities, on this behalf, to a sort of rubber stamp (directives). In recent years EC legislators have developed two tendencies which are on the face of it contradictory but combine in the effect of minimising the influence of national parliaments: (1) very specified and 'technical' norms of harmonisation not allowing for any discretionary powers of member-state legislatures are issued under the heading of 'directive' (instead of regulation, as they ought to). This is done for purely 'cosmetic' reasons: namely, in order to create the impression that the community makes only parsimonious use of binding regulations. (2) The reverse side of the coin is to pass directives which do not contain any details at all but leave it to the non-legislatory procedures of 'comitology' (that is, to the Commission's various committees of 'experts') to settle the more material points of the respective matters.[12] 'Comitology' is one of the more acrimonious bones of contention between the Commission and the European Parliament, its major object being to weaken the EP's part as a co-legislator. In effect, however, it also weakens the member-state parliaments since those details, affixed to the directives, drastically reduce the parliaments' discretionary powers.

Only in matters of EU primary law, i.e., when the treaties are revised, have parliaments decision-making powers worth speaking of. But even then their scope of action amounts to little more than a rubber stamp if they do not want to expose their governments, who take some pains, of course, to convince the public at large that the compromise to be ratified was the utmost that could be obtained in negotiations in the national interest. Consequently, concerning (domestic) European politics parliaments can do little to achieve *ex post* accountability; they are left with hardly any means of control, short of overturning the government. In most countries there is even less they can do *ex ante*. As all observers confirm, governments do not normally 'present policy issues or negotiating stands to national parliaments prior to approval by the Council of Ministers' (Kirchner 1994, p. 260). The only exception

---

12 The impressive number of legislatory and quasi-legislatory decisions on genetically modified organisms, issued since the early nineties and meanwhile a wholly intransparent muddle, may serve as a case in point. The various directives deal with the 'general' question of EU-wide marketing and labelling, etc., while it has been left to committees to decide on which products and for which organisms those rules are to be applied.

to the rule is Denmark (see Norton 1996, p. 110ff.). While the Danish case leaves some doubt as to the feasibility of effective *ex ante* control, the normal course of events is that national parliaments have hardly any other choice than to give the *carte blanche* to their governments. In fact, as some commentators justifiably argue, the 'Danish model' is perhaps not even desirable since it causes 'excessive costs in practical terms (i.e., delays, increasing probability of stalemates etc.)' and tends to 'undermine' the smooth working of European decision-making (Falkner/ Nentwich 1995, 103, 100).

Recognising that there was a problem which needed to be seen to, the European governments added two *Declarations* – No. 13 and No. 14 – to the Maastricht Treaty's Final Act (1992) which were designed as a sort of palliative for national parliaments: they allow for contacts between national members of parliament and the EP and even for joint conferences (*assises*) of the two 'to meet as necessary'. Unfortunately it was left vague what those were going to do and to what effect. At any rate decision-making powers of whichever sort are explicitly excluded.

Although serious enough, the deficits listed may on the whole be judged to be not much different from the day-to-day problem of control cropping up in all parliamentary systems whenever governance is taking the shape of negotiation and 'joint policy making' (as is the case mainly in federalist and in corporatist systems as well as, pervasively, in industrial policy). Hence critics of the de-parliamentarising effects of EU policy making on member states would have to prove that, in fact, either quantitatively or qualitatively a new stage had been reached. Such proof requires some cross-national empirical research which apparently has not yet been undertaken. There is, however, a systematic side of the matter related to the problem of constitutional incompatibilities dealt with here. It is the member-state governments which are the main legislators in the community. Add to this the continuous expansion of community legislative powers *vis-à-vis* the member states and you see EU member countries gradually return to a pre-democratic polity where the executive regains a monopoly of legislation, no longer bound by the representatives of the people. Examining this state of affairs from below, one may conclude that the peoples of member countries are partly 'subjects' of the EU (as a consequence of 'direct effect') and to the same degree robbed of their quality as 'citizens', both at home and in the EU (see Weiler 1996, p. 522). Contrary to the view expressed by the German

Constitutional Court in the Maastricht ruling, this renders current EU policy making incompatible with the constitutional imperatives of political responsibility and of democracy – not only in Germany but in most member states.

As to the other side of the coin of 'post-parliamentarianism' – the shift of power to more or less non-governmental policy networks – the 'new quality' reached at European level seems obvious enough on an empirical basis. We have already noted that the uneven and asynchronous allocation of decision-making powers between the community's formal institutions have triggered off a trend to (pre-)decide over policies in informal circles, typically combining Commission experts and lobbyists. This trend has accelerated as the European policy arena has become more important. It reached a first peak in 1987 when majority voting was introduced into European decision-making. At that point 'lobbying in Europe appears to have exploded' as researchers have found out: 'The EU system is now more lobby-oriented than any national European system' (Andersen & Eliassen 1996, p. 232f.). Since then, at the latest, policy making via specialised policy networks has become the dominant form of European politics. Again, this development has its specific constitutional value, aggravating the incompatibility established above: policy making between administrators and lobbyists is essentially based on 'self-representation' and therefore in conflict with the traditional notion of democratic representation (which includes the idea of a balance between interests and the *bonum commune*), and it precludes accountability to a larger public. It violates fundamental constitutional principles of member states in so far as the citizens are subjected to those policies but have had no say in them whatsoever.

Conclusion

To sum up: (1) With the establishment of the principle of supremacy of community law the EC/EU clashes with (some) member states' governing constitutional principles in so far as they include notions of sovereignty. (2) Realisation of the Single Market touches on various (if not most) policy areas; hence the treaty's in-built teleology precludes a clearly defined (to say nothing of restrictive) allocation of competences. Since this implies that competences allocated at regional level in member states are in no way protected against encroachment by the community, the EU super-structure is not compatible with member-state federalist structures. (3) Policy making in Europe is characterised by a heavy executive bias. In casting governments in the role of legislators, it alters the balance of power between governments and parliaments in member states. Lack of parliamentarisation at European level is followed up by de-parliamentarisation at member-state level. Thus EU politics conflict sharply with the latter's domestic democratic principles.

At first sight, the incompatibility (1) appears to be as incurable as it is unavoidable. A second look reveals that remedies to the incompatibilities (2) and (3) will considerably alleviate the first. As to remedies to the second, it has been suggested that community powers should be applied '*autonomieschonend*' (Scharpf 1994b), i.e., in a way that respects the autonomous status of regional subunits. Such a demand sounds as 'deliciously vague' as the concept of subsidiarity (Weiler 1996, p. 529). The regions' autonomy could be safeguarded more effectively by firmly linking any expansion of community powers not only to the consent of member-state governments but to the consent of subunits too – a device which, incidentally, ought to preclude any further 'creeping' expansion by way of ECJ rulings. As regards the third incompatibility, an obvious yet debatable way of reducing the 'executive bias' and of enabling the principle of democratic self-government to survive in member societies would be the inclusion of national parliaments – or national MPs – into EU decision-making.[13] It is with these and other possible solutions to the problems of incompatibility that the remainder of this book will deal.

---

13 As has been suggested by the French Senate's Guéna Report, 1995. See also (*inter alia*) Laufer & Fischer 1996; Brittan 1994.

3

INADEQUATE SOLUTIONS

The Recent Reform Debate

Seen from the angles of logic and structure, the European polity
has developed in an entirely haphazard and piecemeal fashion. No
plans whatsoever had been drawn up before its birth as regards the
shape of the future political roof of the common market, not to
mention 'constitutional' concepts. Instead, at crucial points in the
EC's history the original layer of intergovernmental cooperation
was complemented with one or the other community institution to
form an additional layer of organisation. These new layers were
not necessarily synchronised with the previous one(s). Apparently
nobody paid much attention as to whether and how the various
layers and elements would connect and whether any of these
additions might not develop its own logic and push the community
in directions not intended by the 'masters of the treaty'.[1]

This state of 'lack of structural considerations' has changed
profoundly in recent years – probably due (1) to the 'new logic'
following from the Single European Act and the introduction of
majority voting in the Council, and (2) to a fact that clearly took
Euro-politicians by surprise: the conspicuous drop of public
support for European integration since the late 1980s (see Reif
1995). One should not forget a third factor, although it sounds
rather trivial: the proliferation of European institutions (and
groups) quite naturally multiplies the number of constitutional
topics to be discussed between them. Whatever the reasons, we are
now confronted with quite an impressive tableau of models and
proposals from official as well as academic sources concerning the

---

1   In the early years of the EC there were, of course, some academics and even
    some politicians dreaming of a future European Federation: the 'United States of
    Europe'. They were not heeded, however, and their plans were lost in oblivion.

future structure of the EU and its 'constitution'. It should not come as a surprise, though, that the need for the latter is still one of the most controversial issues of all.[2] Characteristically, most of those papers were prepared after Maastricht which triggered both hopes and fears. Their aim was to influence the 1996 IGC, to block or to broaden the path to 'federal' and democratic structures.

Recent reform proposals cover a broad range of issues and differ even more in radicality, varying between fundamental change and marginal alterations. Proposals issued by more or less official sources are of course to be found at the latter end of the scale, while one of the most radical variants – a draft version of a European constitution – was submitted by an academic circle of fairly orthodox economists calling themselves the 'European Constitutional Group' (ECG).[3] There are, however, exceptions to the rough correlation of 'official and marginal' on the one hand and 'academic and radical' on the other, witness the EP's Herman Report of 1994 which also includes a draft constitution. Likewise, a bit more on the audacious side are some of the proposals coming from official (or 'half-official') member-state sources, as for instance the French Senate's Guéna Report. Not all of the circulating plans and concepts will (and can) be dealt with in this chapter, nor will all of the proposed institutional changes be discussed. Suffice it here to give a short overview[4] over the key issues of reform, to concentrate then on those which are meant to deal with the incompatibilities outlined above.

(1) As has just been noted, one of the prime bones of contention is the question of whether or not to have such a thing as a constitution at all. Debate on this issue is (in part) so heated because it is closely connected with that of the future character of the Union: state or non-state. Related to this paramount question is how to deal with the 'second and third pillar' (the common foreign and security policy, justice and home affairs) – are they already to be included in a constitutional framework? Another related question is that of the Union's flexibility, for it is difficult to see how a European constitutionalism could be reconciled with a

2 See for the main arguments: Philip Morris Institute 1996, *Does Europe Need a Constitution?*
3 A European Constitutional Settlement. Draft Report by the European Constitutional Group, September 1993. For a short summary see Vibert 1994. I shall repeatedly return to their ideas.
4 For greater detail see Falkner & Nentwich 1995.

practice of 'Europe à la carte' or one of 'variable geometries'. As Falkner and Nentwich (1995, p. 59) indicate, 'a certain opinion leadership' exists for models of the latter type, which makes a hard case for constitutionalists.

(2) A second major issue is the relationship between Union and member states or, in terms of federalism, the allocation of competences between both. In this question a clear demarcation line divides community institutions and 'others'. The former either unabashedly claim the full *Kompetenz-Kompetenz* for the Union's legislators (thus the EP's Aguirre Report of 3 February 1993) or cautiously concede (as does an EP resolution of 17 May 1995) that it might just be conceivable to make use of the 'implied powers' granted by Art. 235 TEC only as a last resort; or they ignore the problem altogether. In contrast, most of the other sources more or less strongly advocate a strict, enumerative list of Union competences.

(3) Probably the majority of proposals deal with the EP – its composition, the weighting of member states' electorates and, particularly, its powers. The demand that the EP's legislative powers ought to be extended is widely endorsed. Even the Commission's 'Task Force' to prepare the IGC agreed that the limitation of co-decision to certain policy areas is 'erratic' and should be removed. Official documents, though, tend to restrict the proposed reform to a mere 'simplification and clarification' (as does, *inter alia*, the Report of the Reflection Group of 1995). Agreement ends abruptly where the EP's powers of election are concerned. More radical proposals – including, of course, those from the EP itself – suggest that the President of the Commission be elected and even nominated by the EP. Furthermore, they wish for the EP's greater influence on the choice of the other members of the Commission as well as on nominations to the Union's courts and to the Board of the European System of Central Banks. Such plans are most strongly opposed by all those who try to stem the (alleged) avalanche towards a European super-state. It is interesting to note that one of the most elaborate constitutional drafts, that of the ECG, is also opposed to the EP's electing the President of the Commission – on the simple ground that it does not envisage the Commission but the Council becoming the European 'government'.

(4) Concepts that assign the role of the future government to the Commission tend to advocate bi-cameralism, with the Council cast in the role of Upper Chamber. Yet views on who is to form the second chamber vary. The ECG, for instance, wants to flank the directly elected EP by a chamber of national parliamentarians.

(5) Depending on the role envisaged for Council and Commission, respectively, reform proposals differ concerning their composition, including the number of commissioners: is it really necessary to have every member state represented in this institution? They also differ regarding their internal structure, their presidencies (elected, rotating, etc.) and most of all regarding their voting procedures: unanimity, majority or the 'double majority' both of states and of total population. Recommendations on this head tend to be very detailed.

(6) Several proposals suggest multi- instead of bi-cameralism, mostly starting from the demand to upgrade the Committee of the Regions (CoR). Interestingly enough, the CoR itself is rather modest in this respect, refraining from claiming legislatory powers for itself. More far-reaching are the requests made by the regions' associations and especially those coming from German sources. Again, the ECG's suggestions are of special interest: although providing only for an advisory role of the CoR, they propose to invest it with certain veto powers. Another variant of additional chamber is that of an assembly of national MPs, which crops up in various guises and comes from various sources (including French and British ones).[5]

(7) The loss of the national parliaments' powers of control has inspired other concepts of providing 'institutional links between the EP and the national parliaments' (Williams 1990, 315), of the *assises* mentioned above or simply of domestic parliamentary reforms (in the wake of the 'Danish model').

(8) Finally, several proposals advocate new or altered reviewing institutions – such as a special European 'Court of Review' (ECG) comprised of judges of the member states' constitutional courts (or their equivalents) or a quite similarly devised 'Constitutional Council' (Weiler 1996, 532).

This picture of manifold issues of and approaches to reform is far from complete, leaving out, for instance, all proposals dealing specifically with the 'second and third pillar' or organisational

5   See the Guéna Report of 1995 in particular; Brittan 1994.

questions of the Monetary Union. Even so it indicates that the Single Market is barely halfway completed and the overarching Union hardly founded, when a pungent need for the reform of both of them makes itself felt. No doubt this is due to the fact that meanwhile the 'ever closer union' is coming 'ever closer' to everybody. Apparently the inherent teleology of the treaties, having gathered new momentum in Maastricht, has been driven forcibly home now to rank and file politicians and even to citizens. The most radical suggestion of reformers, therefore, is perhaps the one made by the ECG to 'delete' the words 'ever closer Union' in Art. A Maastricht Treaty. The reason they give is likely enough: 'a constitutional document should not imply a one way dynamic' (ECG 1993, 'Amendments', p. 2). All non-official proposals, though, are motivated by similar fears: (1) that this new Union might come too close to a super-state (and a fairly centralistic one, into the bargain), and/or (2) that this super-state, while devaluing the member countries' democratic structures and impeding their 'self-government', might allow for too little participation and might be lacking in democratic character. At the same time community officials are haunted by a third fear: that too much consideration both for democratic niceties and for member states' touchiness might severely damage the EC institutions' capacity to cope with community problems efficiently (a problem aggravated when Europe will be further enlarged).

Subsequently I am going to deal mainly with answers to the second fear. Concentrating on the three main strands of the reform debate, parliamentarisation, multi-cameralism and federalisation, I shall attempt to demonstrate that these are not adequate ways to solve the problems of incompatibility and the legitimatory gap properly.

Parliamentarisation

The Present Role of the European Parliament

Full parliamentarisation seems to be the panacea of many (if not of most) would-be reformers. Commission officials, on the other hand, give it as their private view that in this respect an optimum has already (or nearly) been reached. Should any further reform be considered necessary, the matter would be one of scope rather than of principle, of consolidation rather than of extension; for according to this view, the EP is endowed with 'the full range of parliamentary powers'. In fact, the Single European Act (SEA) and the Maastricht Treaty extended the EP's powers considerably, inventing as a first step the process of 'cooperation' (with Council and Commission) and as a second that of 'co-decision' (with the Council). Most commentators agree that the EP in the 1990s owns 'a clear and growing role in the legislative and budgetary process' of the Union, 'plays an important part in the choice of the EU's executive body, the Commission, and has powers of scrutiny as well' (Smith 1995, p.1).[6] What is debatable, however, is whether it has indeed become 'a key player in European decision-making' (ibid., p. 60). According to the aperçu of an insider, it had once been created 'as an afterthought', as a purely consultative or even decorative assembly, annexed to the decision-making system properly. Its critics feel that this character of an annexe or 'afterthought' not entirely fitted into the logic of the system in a way sticks to it still.

This is why authors of reform proposals tend to enumerate the powers the EP does not have, rather than those it has. The list of the former is quite as impressive as the list of the latter, starting with the lack of the (formal) right of initiative which still rests exclusively with the Commission. A second major deficit is that its legislative powers are rather narrowly circumscribed (see Art. 189 ECT). Not only is the EP a mere co-legislator, it is not really on par with the original legislator, the Council, which decides on all community matters while the EP's right of co-decision is (a trifle unsystematically) restricted to certain areas and types of decision (namely, though not exclusively, to those questions where the Council may decide with qualified majority). Although the Amsterdam summit of June 1997 (the final event of the 1996 IGC) increased the number of policy areas subjected to co-decision by about a dozen, they are still 'enumerated' and hence restricted. The asymmetry between the two legislators, Council and EP, thus remains basically intact. But irrespective of statutory rights, the scope of the EP's legislatory powers are reduced by the above-mentioned practice of 'comitology'. The legislatory acts in which the EP participates are frequently confined to mere statements of principles, while it is left to the Commission, the advisory committees of 'experts' attached to it (filled with scientists, government officials and lobbyists in varying composition) and finally to the Council to decide over the more interesting bits – the

6 For a detailed description see Westlake 1995.

details. With regard to them, the EP and its own respective committees are informed and may give their comments which are, however, not binding; and even these poor substitutes for a participation in European legislation were granted only lately, in the *modus vivendi* agreed upon by the EP, the Council and the Commission on 20 December 1994.

Another aspect of the persisting weakness of the EP in its dealings with the main legislator, the Council, is that EP decisions in the complicated co-decision procedure have to be taken by an absolute majority of members, a qualification difficult to be met in the normal course of events due to the present fragmented state of the parliament. Not even the budgetary rights – the third deficit – are fully developed. Although the EP may after a lengthy process reject the EC budget with a majority of two-thirds of the votes cast (Art. 203), the Commission is still entitled to overrule this decision in cases of 'obligatory' expenditure, i.e., which does 'necessarily result from this Treaty' (Art. 204). The obligatory expenditure consists in its better part of the agricultural subsidies which in their turn form the bulk of overall European spending. The fourth deficit usually named is that the EP can reject the incoming Commission only as a whole and has no influence on nominations.

While it ought to be borne in mind that parliaments in some member countries (in France, to name an example) do not have any more powers than the EP has, the role and position of the EP can be summed up as (1) mainly reactive and (2) that of a veto institution: wherever the EP is endowed with 'real' powers, these are blocking powers.

Some reformers from within the community institutions, such as the Commission's Task Force for the preparation of the IGC, tend to join forces with the EP and agree that some of these deficits should and could be remedied. Co-decision at least ought to be extended to 'any area of a legislative nature' – a concession leaving some doubt, however, in a policy making setting renowned for its extensive use of 'comitology' in the grey area between legislation and implementation, as to what precisely a legislative area is. The main object of these inside reformers has been a sort of streamlining of the EP's legislatory role: simplifying the various procedures or at least reducing their number, an object partly achieved at the end of the IGC.

However, alterations such as these hardly sound impressive. At any rate they do not represent 'first steps' towards a fully-fledged parliamentary system which implies apart from full legislatory and budgetary rights full electoral powers of the EP and the unequivocal responsibility of the Union's executive, i.e., the Commission, to the EP. This is what many outside reformers[7] as well as a considerable number of MEPs dream of. As Eurobarometer polls tell us it is also what a majority of European citizens – and the élites, in particular – wish for. In one of its latest surveys the Eurobarometer reports an overall of 65 per cent of élite members (in politics, administration, business and labour, media and 'culture') who endorse the notion of 'a European government responsible to the European Parliament', with even Great Britain scoring as high as 43 per cent.[8] Support of 'normal citizens' for the same issue amounted to 54 per cent (in 1993). One may, however, well wonder about the relevance of these figures, considering the low interest voters display in EP elections. Not only is turnout here low everywhere compared with national elections, but it has even been decreasing.[9] It seems that citizens wish for a 'legitimate' Union but prefer not to legitimise it themselves.

The Absent Demos

Contrary to those obviously common beliefs just noted, there is good reason to believe that the full parliamentarisation of the EU is not only unlikely but not even desirable. At any rate, it is not an adequate solution to the EU's complex legitimatory problem. One argument frequently brought forward against it is the 'No-Demos thesis'. As especially prominent German students of constitutional law (including the Constitutional Court) argue,[10] it is not sufficient to establish a representative body in order to create 'democracy'. Representative institutions and parliamentary majority rule work well and provide for the democratic legitimisation of government only under the condition that they are based on a collective entity called 'the people' or 'the nation', united by a common language, a common culture, common traditions. Such a 'collective identity' is lacking in Europe, and will be lacking for a long time to come.

7   It is interesting to note that in the international political scientists' debate on Europe's future it is particularly the British who advocate clear-cut parliamentarisation.

8   Eurobarometer: Top Decision-makers Survey, Summary Report, September 1996, p. 9. For citizens' opinions see Reif 1993, p. 51, and 1995.

9   From 63 per cent in 1979 down to 56.4 per cent in 1994, on an EU average. The figures would be much lower, were it not for those countries where voting is obligatory. The decline is particularly drastic in the Netherlands where turnout dropped from 57.8 to 35.6 per cent. See Jacobs et al. 1995, p. 29.

10 See Isensee 1994; Grimm 1994; BVerfG 1993.

Where it is absent, no 'public opinion' (in the 'classical' sense; see Habermas 1962, for instance) can emerge; and without public opinion, representative government lacks basis and substance. Parliamentary debates and decisions will then (as likely as not) be miles apart from the wishes and demands of the populace; that is, they are pointless, or mere symbolism.

This thesis is open to criticism when combined with the notions of nationality and ethnicity. Such a linkage represents too narrow a view of the complex process of 'nation-building', both historically and systematically, and over-stresses the degree of homogeneity required. If parliamentary government 'is only legitimate ... when Danes rule Danes' (Weiler 1996, p. 523),[11] what then qualifies the Dane? Even in a country as small as Denmark the major qualification can neither be language nor ethnicity for (apart from modern 'multi-culturalism') there are Danish citizens speaking German and not too long ago there used to be those who were Greenlanders. One does not have to cite the Swiss example to show that it is possible as well as necessary, from theoretical considerations, to decouple the notions of *demos* and *ethnos*, even those of nationality and citizenship. The latter may build up from the combined legal, political, and social *rights* allotted to individuals in the respective society (Meehan 1993, p. 4ff.), constituting a set of 'shared values' to identify with. From this starting-point one may well argue (as Meehan does, ibid.) that a 'European citizenship' has been emerging in recent years, originating, in particular, from EC social policy and the ECJ's enforcement of European social rights. Such supranational citizenship might not unreasonably be expected gradually to transform Europe's 'multiple demoi' (Weiler 1996, p. 526) into a people sufficiently integrated to allow for *some* parliamentary form of government. However, if these *multiple demoi* are likened to the 'citizenship of the Roman Empire in which citizens were able to appeal to more than one set of enforceable standards when claiming their rights' (Meehan, ibid., p. 2), it becomes doubtful again whether this sort of citizenship, although European, does indeed allow for *normal* parliamentary majority rule at Europe's centre.

Before I come back to this subject, there is the other and more practical aspect of the 'No-Demos thesis' to be considered: the lacking intermediary infrastructure (see Grimm 1994; Grande 1996a, p. 348ff.). One of the essential preconditions of parliamentary government is the existence of a party system to

11 For a more detailed critique see also Weiler et al. 1995, p. 11ff.

organise public opinion, in particular to organise politics along the lines of government and opposition as the major way to make political differences visible to the people. Representative systems need parties to establish a link between politics and the electorate and to hold governments politically resonsible. It is difficult to see how voters could 'punish' a disappointing government without opposition parties providing alternatives.

At present no 'genuine parties' exist on the European scene, 'if by this we mean organisations that span and control the electoral linkage' (Andersen & Eliassen 1996, p. 16). The groups calling themselves European parties are loose confederations of national parties, without an internal organisation to speak of, let alone one reaching down to the 'grass roots', without a proper leadership known and visible to electors, indeed without an electorate of their own. The groupings into which the EP is split are little (if at all) more than alliances of MEPs partly uniting rather strange bedfellows; without a whip, of course, because national parties dominate the scene, even on the floor of the EP. It has been argued that 'genuine' parties would emerge, quasi-automatically, once the EP had an important political task to fulfill (ibid., p. 17). Yet the supervisory powers of the EP, which since Maastricht are *de jure* considerable, have not been effectively used because considerations of national politics have prevailed among the MEPs. The same holds true of the power to confirm the Commission. On the quiet, insiders admit that even where positions within the EP itself are concerned (as, for instance, its presidency), the question is not who might best fill the post but whose turn it is according to the 'balance of powers' of member states. 'Thus the continued dominance of national politics prevented the EP making maximum use of its new powers.' (Smith 1995, p. 75)

The way interest groups operate in Brussels is indicative of the same prevalence of national considerations. In the 1980s some business associations at least achieved a higher degree of Europeanisation than parties (see Andersen & Eliassen 1996, pp. 41-55; Mazey & Richardson 1993). But while such a development was easily attributable to the growing importance of the European policy arena and wholly in line with common theories of interest group behaviour, a new and for most observers rather unexpected trend is to be noted lately: since the SEA, lobbying as a whole has exploded but more specifically so has the lobbying of *national* interest groups in Brussels. Now that national governments seem to be losing in power and importance, the German industries' and employers' peak associations BDI and BDA (for instance) take great care to be present at the emerging new power centre directly and operate next to and not always in accordance with the European federation of industries' associations UNICE, to further their members' interests. Apparently, not nation-*state* interests but national (or territorial) interests thus reassert themselves.[12] The European peak associations, at any rate, are momentarily cast into the shadow.

The Absent Majority

The lack of infrastructure might be judged as a passing phenomenon but the recent reassertion of national interest groups indicates that the territorial dimension of politics is deeply embedded in people's minds and will not lose its salience in the foreseeable future. This leads us to the major reason why full parliamentarisation will not be the solution to the EU's legitimatory problems. The 'European society' is extremely heterogeneous – so much so, in fact, that one would rather speak of 'multiple societies'. Primarily it is territorially segmented, the territorial divisions (mostly) coinciding with those of language, culture, political traditions, notions of democracy, and not least those of economic interests. At the European level, all the territorial entities have the status of minorities. Since no genuine 'European majority' (defined by 'Europeanness', class, hegemonic country or whatever) exists, there seems to be, on the face of it, little danger of all these minorities becoming structural ones (i.e., becoming marginalised, their interests permanently ignored). A continually high fluctuation of coalitions between them, giving every minority the chance to have its interests attended to every now and then, is on the other hand a purely accidental outcome. There is no safeguard against being frequently outvoted and thus being cast into the role of structural minority for any of them, if decisions at the European centre are taken by simple majority as is the normal practice in parliamentary democracy. Its majoritarian logic precludes systematic consideration of minority concerns. The dangers linked to such neglect will arouse the more fears, the more the decisions at the centre infringe on territories' right of self-government and the more they are (or appear to be) irreversible.

---

12 For the continued importance of national interest groups and national channels of lobbying see Mazey & Richardson 1993, p. 27ff.

The inadequacy of representative and parliamentary government in a society as heterogeneous as the European one is aggravated by the fact that the EP is by nature, i.e., following its self-interest, the major agent of integration next to the Commission.[13] In plain words: the MEPs' interest lies in accumulating decision-making powers at the top, since this enhances their own importance. Incidentally, this is one of the reasons why the EP has up to now so rarely used its blocking powers: MEPs 'do not want to be seen as putting a break on Community legislation' (Smith 1995, p. 83). In terms of federalism, the parliament thus operates as a centralising agency, a trend that coincides with the evidence borne out in virtually all federations. What matters to federal parliaments are their own rights as a legislative body, not those of subunits or of minorities.[14] Being led by a majority supporting the government, they will tend to be less opposed to the executive than to the federal chamber. In the European context this means cooperating with the Commission and being critical towards the Council and its members' vetoing powers.

Other heterogeneous societies have developed specific forms of democracy which differ from majoritarian parliamentarianism. Whether these are called 'consociationalism' or 'Konkordanz-' or consensus democracy (Lijphart 1984), they are all based on the same principle of not outvoting any of the society's segments (or 'pillars') but of giving their élites a share in the power at the centre (or top). In a way the EU at present resembles such a consociationalist or 'pillarised' system (see Christiansen 1995; Weiler et al. 1995, p. 28ff.). Its territorial segments – the member states – are closely integrated at the top, i.e., via their governments who take great care not to get outvoted (although, as recent history shows, outvoting does happen). What is lacking is a 'democratic outlet' (Abromeit 1987) to this élite cartel to legitimise the compromises reached in complicated negotiations and to allow for corrections if élites have digressed too far from their 'pillars'' interests in the process. Such an outlet is not to be found in parliamentarisation. Where segments differ as dramatically as they do in Europe, and the people's primary allegiance rests with the

13 Especially where ideology is concerned, the EP may even be judged to be the 'institution most committed to the objective of the European Union' (Williams 1990, p. 301).

14 '...the majoritarian logic that characterises parliamentary systems tends to promote the development of a horizontal rationality within the central institutions ... This clearly does not simplify relationships between the various levels of power' (Dehousse 1995, p. 129).

segments, a parliament's majoritarian decisions cannot but produce resentment and thus have disintegrative effects. For even if Danes might not think twice about being ruled solely by Danes, they would most strongly object to being outvoted by Germans, Swedes, Britons and suchlike. As keen observers already note, 'the increased influence of the Parliament ... has added layers to the process [of decision-making, H.A.], but has not provided a firm basis for legitimising European politics.' (Wallace 1996, p. 66). Upgrading it further would in fact rather de-legitimise them.

Multi-Cameralism

The same effect – further complicating the system without legitimising it – is to be expected from the device to enrich it with additional representative chambers. Two variants have been suggested: a committee or 'Senate' composed of national MPs and a 'Senate of Regions'. A precursor of the latter has come into existence by now in the shape of the Committee of the Regions (CoR) but is considered to be in need of upgrading. If we assume for the moment that the Council will be transformed into an Upper House, then both variants would figure as third or fourth chambers. Their rationale would be to fill the legitimatory gaps which in the first case result from the shift to qualified majority voting (QMV) in Council decision-making and in the second case from the transfer of competences from member states' subunits to the community. Both are deemed to solve the Union's incompatibility problems that have been described above.

The Regional and the Parliamentarians' Chamber

A brief look at the present CoR will help to clarify its inherent weaknesses,[15] some of which might give a clue to those of multi-cameralism in general. The idea of establishing a regional representation in Brussels had been pushed particularly by the German Länder. Their eagerness was due to their dissatisfaction with SEA negotations from which they had been entirely excluded. The result of these negotiations made them fear that under QMV further inroads would be made into the remainder of policy making under their own, or at least under domestic, jurisdiction. The associations formed by regions (Assembly of the Regions,

15 For a brief description see Onestini 1994.

Europe of the Regions[16]), which have sprung up since the mid-1980s, were the other advocates of the concept of regional representation. Massively supported by the German government, the concept was eventually included in the Maastricht Treaty, though somewhat watered down, of course, since it was to the same extent opposed by unitary states such as the U.K. Characteristically, British politicians warned that such a regional Committee would be 'the nucleus of a new unitary state in Europe'.[17]

The first practical problem that cropped up regarding this new institution, was how it ought to be composed. At that time only two of the member states were federations with autonomous subunits; two (Italy and Spain) had taken some steps towards regionalisation and had granted half-autonomous status to some regions. The other member countries were unitary states of varying degrees of centralisation, with regions that are ancient provinces, economic areas or simply geographical units. Hence, a common denominator had to be found for regions or territories of such unequal character. The answer to the puzzle was (a) to combine regional and local representation, (b) to allot seats according not to the actual number of *Länder*, provinces or regions, but to the weight of member states in the other European institutions, and (c) to leave it to member states how to choose the nominees then to be appointed by the Council (Art. 198 a TEC). The whole package caused considerable problems within member countries. The Germans, for instance, wondered how to distribute the twelve of their twenty-four seats reserved for the 'regions' between the sixteen *Länder*, while the British witnessed a heated debate about the question whether their twenty-four delegates had to be locally elected or could be appointed by the government without any (formal) consideration of local or regional interests. As a result, a regional representation has been added to the community institutions the representative character of which is very much in doubt.

Moreover, the heterogeneity of its members – in domestic status as well as concerning the 'basis' they represent – is bound to lead to severe internal conflict. Local representatives stand against

16 The former comprises about 300 regions, including those of non-member states; the latter (founded in reaction to the first and, again, spearheaded by the German *Länder*) confines itself to regions of member states.
17 The Rt. Hon. William Cash in a House of Commons Debate; House of Commons Records 1993, p. 1029. Quoted in: Dehousse & Christiansen 1995, p. 37.

regional ones (and can even outvote the latter[18]), industrial areas against rural regions, the North against the South, government officials against elected politicians. To make matters worse, CoR members belonging to the European Socialist Party and the European People's Party meet 'privately' before plenary sessions, trying to adopt German practices of grouping into '*A-* and *B-Länder*'[19] and to subject regional interests to party politics. With a fragmented body such as this it is difficult to make one's voice heard and to have it taken seriously by other institutions.

Hence the insiders' observation that the CoR is predominantly 'occupied with itself' – which is perhaps as well since there is little else for the Committee to do. For the second problem of the CoR is its lack of powers: it is a purely consultative body and 'may' be heard but is not necessarily listened to. Although advice from the Committee is mandatory in a number of cases (such as education and culture, trans-European networks, Structural Funds and environmental issues; see Articles 126ff. TEC), an obligation for the Council and the Commission to wait for the CoR's statement, let alone heed it, can at best be implied; and there are no sanctions if both fail to do so. The most urgent of the reform demands issued by the Committee itself therefore is the right to take Commission or Council to Court if the Committee feels itself unjustly ignored.

In practice both the CoR's heterogeneity and its lack of power have led to lasting disillusionment amongst its members; in particular, the German *Länder's* prime ministers, who had taken great care to be appointed in the beginning, are rather loth by now to attend the sessions. Now they dispatch junior civil servants from their chancelleries. Disillusionment seems to reign on the side of the European executive as well: the administration of the Structural Funds, for instance, goes largely past the CoR; their planning as well as their implementation is dealt with bilaterally between officials from the responsible Directorate(s) General and regional executives. According to Commission insiders, the CoR has after only a few years of its existence already reached the same stage of disregard and of irrelevance which it took the Social and Economic Council twenty years to obtain.

18 110 of the present CoR members are usually classified as local and 112 as regional but of the latter group at least thirty-eight rather belong to an 'intermediary' class, i.e., their 'regional' character is much in doubt. See Dehousse & Christiansen 1995, p. 40; Laufer & Fischer 1996, p. 116f.
19 This jargon has come into use in the 1970s. '*A-Länder*' are those governed by the SPD, '*B-Länder*' those governed by CDU or CSU.

Yet institutions once established tend to survive. Small wonder then that reform proposals are brought forward to lend some sense to the CoR's survival. As has been noted above, the CoR itself is rather modest in its demands. Apparently, it would just like to be listened to. But modesty does not always pay. The majority of the Reflection Group declined a right of the Committee to appeal to the ECJ (see Reflection Group 1995, pt. 123); so that claim was not even put on the IGC's agenda. The above-mentioned regional associations have been more radical in their claims, aiming at a 'Senate of Regions' of equal standing with the EP and asking for the participation of a regional representation in the Union's legislative process. There are those whose dreams reach even further: a 'Europe of the Regions' can also mean that the nation-states, sort of 'sandwiched' between the European and the regional level, dwindle away in political substance and importance. Were this the case, there would be no need to think twice about multi-cameralism, for together with the nation-states the Council would lose its central role and the 'Senate' take over its position as Upper Chamber.

The concept of a Senate is a baffling one, however, for other models envisage it composed of members of national parliaments.[20] Both variants of additional chambers – the regional chamber and the chamber of national parliamentarians – apparently have a common root.[21] Indication for this is not least the rights to be allotted to the latter, which are (according to Brittan 1994, p. 227) (1) the enforcement of subsidiarity, (2) the right to challenge the legal basis on which laws are drafted, (3) scrutiny of all laws carrying the EU into 'new territory' and (4) scrutiny of laws concerning home affairs. In other proposals too, the parliamentarians' chamber would have mainly to deal with the allocation of competences. This is in fact one of the main concerns of subunits in federations, and the raison d'être of federal second chambers.

Additional Chambers and Symbolic Politics

The notion that nation-states are 'sandwiched' and eventually squeezed out of European policy making is flatly unrealistic. Hence the question is not one of a chamber of regions or one of

---

20 Thus, as early as 1989, the then speaker of the Belgian Parliament Ch.-F. Nothomb, and the French Minister of Foreign Affairs, R. Dumas; see Müller-Brandeck-Bocquet 1991, p. 17.

21 Consequently, the ECG's draft constitution allows for alternating membership in the CoR and the Chamber of Parliamentarians; see ECG 1993, 'Main institutions', p. 16.

parliamentarians *replacing* the Council but one of third or fourth chambers *added* to the present triangle of Commission (as an executive), Council (oscillating between the executive and a legislative chamber), and EP (a not very potent legislative chamber). Objections to both proposals are primarily founded on the doubt that there is any practical sense in multi-cameralism. There is no historical evidence for a workable legislative system consisting of more than two chambers. Experiments have been made with social and/or economic councils, added to the normal two-chamber parliament to co-decide in the respective policy areas in various countries (the German Weimar Republic, France, Italy, Belgium, the Netherlands). In most cases these additional institutions have at best been quasi-chambers, more of an advisory character, endowed with little more rights than that of initiative. Wherever they gained political importance (as in the case of Dutch corporatism) they tended to reduce the parliament proper to a mere rubber stamp.[22]

The lesson to be learnt from this experience is that genuine power sharing between more than two chambers is extremely rare; it is difficult enough between two of them. The likeliest course of events is that the additional chamber issues (more or less expert) statements, to be heeded or not.[23] When in some or all policy areas equal rights are formally granted to the additional chamber, the case (second likeliest) will be one of the additional chamber rubber-stamping the decisions of the 'normal' legislative chamber(s) – or vice versa. In the unlikely case of both having the same blocking power, actual decision-making will pass to informal bodies. Hence the decision-making system as a whole will lack transparence; responsibilities will be fatally and continually blurred.

In the European context another aspect must be considered. The ambiguous status of the CoR members coming from unitary states will in the last resort make them cling to their 'national' interest. In controversial matters they will tend to act as an additional representation of the member states – mostly even of their governments (the more so the more they depend on the latter for their appointment). The effect of the mere multiplication of nation-state representation and of doubling of what happens in

22 This even though the Dutch Social-Economic Council was not exactly a 'chamber' but by status rather a consultative body of the government (see Scholten 1987, p. 120ff.). The same experience has been made in Austria where the *Paritätische Kommission* is, however, entirely informal (see Luther & Müller 1992).
23 Reflecting this, the ECG unequivocally conceptualises the CoR as a purely advisory body to assist the Chamber of Parliamentarians (i.e., the second chamber). See ECG 1993, 'Main institutions', p. 15.

the Council can with still greater certainty be expected from a committee of MPs. While regional representatives might yet try to use the new forum to give a voice to domestic discontent, delegates from national parliaments will mirror, in a more or less distorted manner, the proportionate weight of government and opposition parties; their respective majorities in such a chamber will therefore back their governments.

On the whole, additional chambers like these will have to be judged as superfluous. Certainly there is little additional legitimisation to be gained from their existence – not least for the simple reason that as a rule they will decide by majority vote like any (quasi-) parliamentary chamber. Obtaining their assent will complicate decision-making, but neither any single region, nor any other domestic minority, will achieve protection of their rights and interests from them. Adding further institutions to the top layer of the European polity cannot be the solution to the Union's legitimatory and incompatibility problems. In fact, it is difficult to see how anything else except symbolic politics can accrue from such devices. It means to be both over-optimistic and over-modest to trust in mere symbolic acts to produce gains in legitimacy (and 'at little financial and political cost', too! Christiansen 1995, p. 51) and to reduce discontent at the periphery. 'Going to Brussels' may add status to regional politicians but hardly to regions themselves. Even if the CoR should initially have raised hopes that the EU would indeed come 'closer to citizens' and listen to them, these have long been thwarted for lack of political relevance as well as in this specific case for lack of clear links between CoR members and reference groups at home. The mere pretence of effective representation will now rather enhance discontent.

Federalism

It is widely believed that 'a federalist nation is ... an unfinished nation' (Duchacek 1970, p. 192) though this is neither historically nor theoretically correct. Federalism is rather one of the devices to integrate heterogeneous societies (see above). Hence contrary to the British public's view, federalism does not necessarily sooner or later lead to the unitary state but aims instead to prevent it. There are, however, different types of federations, more 'dual' and more 'interlocking' or 'unitary' ones, and anyone who talks about federalism has a specific type in mind. This is where the manifold misunderstandings between Anglosaxons and Continentals emerge. And of course, great caution is advised whenever politicians talk about federalism and – even worse – when they profess to federalist structures for Europe. This has become quite a fashion since the Maastricht negotiations, as has the recourse to the 'principle of subsidiarity' which is equally open to diverse interpretations: it can mean both the protection of the right of subunits to mind their own business as long as they are able to do so, *and* the right of central institutions to intervene when they are convinced the subunits are not.

The two models of federalism can roughly be sketched as follows: dual federalism is characterised (1) by a division of legislative competences, of administration and of finance between subunit and central level ('concurrent government'); (2) by the participation of subunits in central decision-making by means of an elected chamber, representing them equally and endowed with equal rights to the chamber representing the people as a whole; (3) by a modicum of veto rights of subunits whenever their core interests are at stake. In contrast, unitary federalism knows (1) 'concurring powers' of legislation,[24] shared finance, interlocking administration and, consequently, joint policy making; (2) subunits' participation in central decision-making solely rests with governments, sitting in a sort of second chamber which is not on a par with the parliament and where, furthermore, their votes are weighted (according to population); (3) subunits have little or no veto rights.

The EU: a Case of Creeping Centralisation

As has repeatedly been indicated, the EC has already taken quite a few steps in the direction of unitary federalism (see, for instance, Scharpf 1994a, p. 221f.). Most commentators agree that, with regard to competences, the EC history has up to now been one of 'creeping centralisation'. The treaty does not divide community and member-state competences. Its inbuilt teleology, enforced by the ECJ, as well as the implied-powers clause of Art. 235 TEC (and similar clauses tucked away in some other articles) allow the extension of the vaguely circumscribed and encompassing community powers without necessitating any revision of the treaty. At least in the cases where Art. 235 TEC is explicitly applied member states could halt this development with their veto. Yet

24 Which means the 'competitive' allocation of powers: federation and subunits 'compete' in the same policy areas.

there is little they can do against the way the ECJ shapes the community law and claims a *Kompetenz-Kompetenz* for itself – short of (unanimously, of course) abolishing the Court.

Although the subsidiarity principle of Art. 3 b TEC is intended to silence critics of the steady process of transferring legislative powers from states and regions to the top level, it cannot be expected to serve as a potent restriction of community powers. It is an ambiguous principle that can be read as a protection of states' rights as well as a *carte blanche* for the community. Nor is it enforceable, lacking the precision required to take any of the Union's institutions to Court in the event of violation. The notorious Art. 3 b simply states that 'the Community shall take action' whenever the aims of the intended action 'cannot be sufficiently achieved' by the member states and can be 'better achieved' by the community. It leaves it to the community to decide whether this is the case; and it does not stop to ask whether the 'objectives of the proposed action' themselves are rightfully within the scope of community activity. Understandably, the Commission was rather pleased with this stipulation which is none, at any rate not a restrictive one, and openly declared its intention to use it, when necessary, as a legal permit to extend further its powers.[25] In fact, Art. 3 b should be seen as a mere complement to Art. 235 TEC: 'the latter providing for implied powers, the former specifying the conditions and the way in which they may be exercised' (Rosas/Antola 1995, p. 44). In the lengthy explanation of the subsidiarity principle added to Art. 3 b in the Amsterdam agreement the balance was shifted slightly towards the protection of states' rights (see below, chapter 7). But the basic ambiguity was not altered, nor (probably) the lack of enforceability.

If the allocation of competences is assessed, then there is little doubt that the EC – i.e., the 'first pillar' of the Union – is to be placed on the unitary side of federalism. Matters are more complicated with regard to finance. The 'masters of the treaty' refrained from granting tax autonomy to the community. The Treaty anyhow is extremely reticent on the question of the EC's revenues. These are (1) the common customs duties, plus the agricultural levies (together roughly 25 per cent of EC income in 1992),[26] and (2) the contributions paid by member states, weighted according to their GDP and to their VAT revenues (amounting to 50

25 In a Statement of 27 October 1992 given to Council and EP. After some protest, the Commission revised its stance slightly in a Statement of 24 November 1993.
26 For the figures see Weidenfeld 1995, p. 212.

per cent and 14 per cent respectively); they are periodically fixed in separate budget agreements, usually after fierce battles (witness Mrs Thatcher's crusade for fair shares in the early 1980s, ending with victory in 1984, i.e., a discount on British contributions). The Commission has repeatedly asked for a new own revenue, tax-like and independent of contributions. Not surprisingly, the majority of member states is strongly opposed to such plans, wishing to retain their firm grip on EC finances.

Whereas the revenue side of the EC's financial provisions resembles *con*federalism rather than federalism, the expenditures present a somewhat different picture. In the first place, expenditure growth has been considerable, the EC budget nearly trebling in the decade 1980-90. The Edinburgh agreement of 1992 tried to restrict further growth but could only momentarily stem the tide. While such an 'explosion' of expenditure at the top level is, according to economists, rather typical for federations in general, the second feature – the intense intertwining of expenditures of different levels – is a characteristic of 'interlocking' federalism in particular. This feature has lately gained in importance with the reform and financial extension of the Structural Funds[27] since 1988 and their completion by the Cohesion Funds in 1992. The administration of these Funds resembles the fiscal policies of unitary federations like Germany, not only as regards their fiscal 'combine' (projects are planned, financed and administered jointly) but also their logic of inter-regional distribution: prospering regions (indirectly) subsidise the backward ones.

When we take a look at the representation of member states at community level, we are presented with a similarly ambivalent picture. The Council (as the respective institution) is not exactly of equal standing with the directly elected representation of the people but does clearly dominate. On the other hand, votes in the Council are weighted (if majority voting is applied); members are not treated as equals as is usually the case in confederations as well as in dual federalism. They have, however, retained their veto right in a number of cases.

So, in federalist terms, the overall picture of the EC is anything but clear-cut. It is a mixture of dual and unitary as well as of confederalist elements instead. There seems to be only one historical example with similar traits: the German Empire of 1871 (see Abromeit 1993). Its 'sovereign' was the assembly of princes –

---

27 The European Regional Development Fund ERDF, the European Social Fund ESF, and the European Agricultural Guidance and Guarantee Fund EAGGF.

the *Bundesrat* – which was presided over by the Prussian king under the name of 'German Emperor' (a figure that is missing, so far, in Europe) and managed by a secretary called 'chancellor'. The role of the chancellor and his administration can be compared with that of the Commission today. The *Bundesrat* was the assembly of sovereigns, but not one of equals: as in the Council, their votes were weighted. And although there was a directly elected parliament (the *Reichstag*), it was – like the EP – no fully fledged legislative but shared this role with (and was checked by) the assembled sovereigns. The fiscal situation was similar in that the *Länder* governments took great care to keep the Reich dependent on their *Matrikular*-contributions. Yet both competences and expenditures of the Reich grew continually. At the time, the conglomeration of confederalist, (dual) federalist and unitary elements which characterised the Empire (apart from the Prussian hegemony from which it originated) baffled students of constitutional law. They saw no historical precedent to it; apparently it was wholly 'original' and a type of state *sui generis* (Deuerlein 1972, p. 132) – and in this specific quality a precursor of the European Union.

Federalising a Federation...?

Considering the 'mixed-federal' character of the EU, one may well wonder why so many would-be reformers claim that the community ought to develop 'federalist structures'. Among them, German sources, including a group called *Europäische Struktur-kommission* (ESK), figure prominently. In the run-up to Maastricht the German *Länder*, the *Bundesrat* and the ESK had already expressed their urgent wish for a serious recognition of the subsidiarity principle and for the establishment of a 'federal balance' (see, for instance, Weidenfeld 1991), as well as for a proper representation of the regions. After Maastricht they renewed these demands, justly pointing to the fact that neither had the principle of subsidiarity as formulated in Art. 3 b TEC any tangible meaning, nor had community and member-state competences been sorted out in any way. In their view matters had instead worsened by introducing, now even by primary law, quite a number of new community competences (see Laufer & Fischer 1996, p. 39ff., 84ff.).

Recent reform proposals centre more exclusively around this matter of allocating competences. Their main elements are: (1) generally, a change of the principle of allocation – away from the functional teleology ('completion of the single market') which does not allow for any limitations of community affairs, towards a precise assignment of single competences; and more specifically (2) the abolition of Art. 235 TEC and (3) the firm establishment of a 'catalogue of competences'.[28] Only a few proposals proceed further to demand a cut-back of the financial involvement of the community in regional affairs, i.e., a reform of the Structural Funds.[29] On the other hand, the draft constitution of the EP of 1993[30] allows, under the guise of 'federal structures', community institutions to extend their competences themselves by normal legislation, even against a member state's veto. This would, in fact, render Art. 235 TEC superfluous since it reaches far beyond it.

The concepts both of the ESK and of the EP, concerning 'federalist structures', are modelled after the German variant of interlocking federalism.[31] This implies that they would prolong rather than remove some of the most damaging weaknesses of current European politics. In the first place and contrary to statements of intent they would not put an end to the present ambiguities concerning legislative powers nor to the joint policy making that more or less inevitably results from this. The catalogue of competences submitted by the ESK is only an attempt to clarify their existing distribution, but it does not try to find a plausible (and restrictive) logic for their allocation. Furthermore, by distinguishing 'primary' and 'partial' competences the ESK subcutaneously introduces something like 'concurrent powers' of legislation into European constitutionalism. These are one of the major causes of the unitary character of German federalism for they allow the central level to extend its competences without much ado (see Abromeit 1992a, p. 40ff.). The federal level in Germany may enact legislation in the respective areas whenever this is required by the 'unity of law and economy' or by the necessity to create 'uniform conditions of life' in the Republic (Art. 72 Grundgesetz); whenever it does so, the *Länder* lose their right of legislation in the same areas, i.e., their legislative powers are squeezed. According to the ESK's concept, the European community's 'partial competences' would not be separated from the 'primary competences' of the member states; instead they would invade the latter's territory in a

28 See ESK: Europe 1996 (Weidenfeld 1995, p. 20ff.); Laufer & Fischer 1996, p. 137ff.
29 Thus the Bavarian government, in September 1996.
30 Aguirre Report of 3 February 1993; see Schneider & Wessels 1994, p. 39f.
31 Hesse & Wright 1996 (p. 82ff., 380) argue that German federalism is the appropriate model (1) because of the analogies of the EU structure with some traits of German federalism and (2) because of the latter's success and efficiency (an opinion not shared by all experts, however).

way similar to that just described (though not legally preventing any further legislation by member states on the respective issues, but binding them as regards content). The notion of 'partial competence' would probably tempt the community to round off and complete what is but partial, facing no other (legal) barrier than the principle of subsidiarity which is at least as ineffectual as the stipulation of Art. 72 GG.[32] With its proposal the ESK meant to introduce a 'dual structure' of competences in the sense of 'rule and exception' (Weidenfeld 1995, p. 25); the likely outcome, however, might well be the exception as the rule.

Both the concurring powers and the partial competences have the effect either of centralisation or of forcing the levels of jurisdiction into permanent cooperation: into joint policy making. The deficits of the latter – the lack of transparency, the blurring of responsibilities, as well as its inefficiencies – have been frequently described (see Scharpf 1988). These deficits are especially pronounced where joint decision-making between territorial units or levels is primarily an affair of the executive, which is the case both in Germany and in the EC. Whereas parliamentarians might be trusted to take care that the powers of their unit are not diminished, administrators or government members of the same units cannot be relied upon in this respect – not as long, at least, as they can be sure to retain (or even to gain) a certain influence in bargaining networks: They trade (the unit's) competences against (personal) influence. The second weakness of the described federalist reform proposals therefore is that they do not even attempt to make amends for the existing executive bias of EU policy making. They may have been blinded to its negative consequences by the conviction that the German model is worth being copied; or they may have skipped them because this bias – firmly rooted in the Council – cannot be altered, anyway.

Alternative Models

Hence it is doubtful whether the federalist reforms proposed are worth this name. In order to amend a polity which in formal structure resembles the German Empire and as regards actual

32 Scharpf, in fact, does not even think it reasonable to provide for 'reserved powers' of member states because of the general interdependence of policies and, as a consequence, state and community tasks (in: Weidenfeld 1995, p. 83ff.; see also Scharpf 1994a, p. 226). His idea of a 'bipolar' instead of a 'unipolar logic' of allocation, specifying and enumerating the competences of *both* levels of legislation with equal emphasis is, however, worth considering (Scharpf 1994a, p. 224).

policy making the Federal Republic, proposals drawing from the latter model are at any rate more than modest, envisaging only marginal change. Other models and concepts do exist but receive little attention. The historical example of a 'union of states', the U.S.A., has only perfunctorily been dwelt upon, although various aspects of the American federalism of the nineteenth century – the doctrine of 'dual sovereignty' and the resulting dual structure of state organisation and restrictive view of federal competences, the openness for new states still to be founded,[33] even Calhoun's idea of 'concurrent majorities' – might be worth looking at more closely. Only the last named notion has found its way into the debate, in the shape of a voting system of double majorities (of member states and of populations) in a reformed Council. Apart from this, (modern) American federalism in the eyes of would-be reformers is primarily identified with a strong federal level, with an extensive administration of its own, its powers boosted by the Interstate Commerce Clause, the implied powers doctrine and the practice of 'categorical grants', with the states' rights safeguarded by little else than an ominous 'political process'.[34]

The other 'classical' federation, Switzerland, is even less recognised as a model for the design of a European constitution. This is the more surprising as the Swiss managed to keep the dual structure of their federation in this century largely intact. Neither competences nor finances have been concentrated at the centre (see Abromeit & Pommerehne 1992). Although federal legislation has expanded (albeit not much, compared with other federations), it is strictly confined to guidelines, elaborated upon, thereafter, by cantonal law. All *Kantone* are regarded as equals and their rights safeguarded against federal majorities in a way sometimes reaching (in the eyes of domestic critics) beyond what is to be borne in a democracy. Furthermore, Switzerland is the rare example of successful integration of a heterogeneous society, divided by language, ethnicity, and religion – in fact, the example of a state made up of 'multiple demoi'. European commentators tend to skip this latter aspect because of its historical 'uniqueness' which cannot be copied. At the same time, they disqualify the federalist structure and the specific system of 'half-direct-democratic' decision-making

---

33 See for this the Northwest Ordinance of 1787, guaranteeing the greatest possible amount of freedom for the future member states as regards their internal organisation. The only stipulation was that human rights had to be safeguarded.

34 The Supreme Court, in Garcia v. San Antonio Metropolitan Transit Authority, 1985. For a critical comment see Conlan 1990.

as essentially anachronistic and inadequate for problem-solving in modern societies, particularly for a regulative economic community like the EC. In this, European reformers have apparently listened too intently to Swiss domestic critics and to their lasting lament over Swiss immobilism and of the 'Helvetian malaise' (Imboden 1962). There are only a few observers who agree with the principle underlying Swiss pragmatism: not all the matters which on the face of them cry for 'harmonisation' do at closer inspection indeed call for central action (see Blöchliger & Frey 1992, p. 540f.). There are even fewer to make this principle one of the cornerstones of a reform proposal as the ECG do who emphasise the need to invent devices against creeping centralisation and to put fetters on community competences.

Conclusion

Where federalism is concerned, we end up with the paradox that in the European reform debate the dual, 'classical' models are rejected, mainly on the grounds that federations are states, anyway, and tend to become more unitary over the years – or not, which makes them inefficient. At the same time, political practice proceeds along the lines of the unitary, interlocking model, without apparent compunction. 'Realistic' reform proposals therefore concentrate on the latter model no matter how state-like the original may be and content themselves with minor improvements.

Concerning the 'democratic deficit', reform proposals tend to be more radical yet less realistic, in advocating bi-cameralist parliamentarianism. Again, these proposals are drawn from the 'wrong model', which is the comparatively homogeneous nation-state. The model is wrong because it does not reflect the multi-level and multi-dimensional character of European politics, because it is oblivious of the role the nation-states desperately try to retain, and because it ignores the (cultural) heterogeneity of the member societies. Accordingly, adherence to it will not lead to the bridging of the legitimatory gap which has opened up in Europe. The democratic deficit is not primarily one of lacking institutions; in fact, the architects of the Union have erred rather on the other side, in inventing too many of them. More than new – or strengthened – institutions are necessary to remove it. This is why it would be also unwise to place one's hope in additional chambers such as the CoR or a Chamber of Parliamentarians.

Other devices are needed to provide for the democratic
legitimisation of EU policy making. If we do not get any plausible
answers from common European notions of representative
democracy (federalist or not), we have to look elsewhere: for
devices that (1) do not depend on statist organisation, (2) do not
require additional institutions, (3) allow for different political
traditions to survive and coexist, but (4) make participation of
citizens at the peripheries in community decision-making possible.
Extremely few would-be reformers have hit upon the idea that this
complex puzzle might be solved by the introduction of elements of
direct democracy into the European polity.[35] At the official level,
the Austrian and the Italian delegations to the IGC in October 1996
submitted the proposal to include citizens into the legislative
process, by allowing public petitions (to be heeded as soon as
citizens of at least three member states have combined). It was not
at all likely that any such proposals would be adopted by the IGC
but this may well be the path on which adequate solutions to the
EU's legitimatory problems are to be found.

35 See the group 'Eurotopia' and Erne et al., 1995; Zürn 1996; Grande 1996a;
Nentwich 1998.

4

IN SEARCH OF AN ADEQUATE MODEL:

THEORETICAL CONSIDERATIONS

The reform proposals discussed so far have been drawn either from the widespread model of (majoritarian) parliamentary democracy or from models deemed particularly successful (such as German federalism). In part they have tried to add, in a more or less piecemeal fashion, new elements to those 'common' models (adding up, mainly, to multi-cameralism), without spending much thought on the question of whether or not such additions might alter the logic of the model altogether. Their failure to produce an adequate solution to the EU's legitimatory and compatibility problems may suggest proceeding in a more systematic way. Consequently, my search for an adequate concept will start with a fresh look at the theories underlying democratic practice, as well as with a perusal of several strands of contemporary political theory, in the hope of eliciting from this exercise one or the other useful notion about how a complex and heterogeneous non-state like the EU might be 'constitutionalised'.

Incidentally, such a theoretical survey (however brief) is the more advisable as our problem is not just one of practical politics but also one of democratic theory. The fact that political science has so far contributed surprisingly little that is of use for the solution of the riddle is not least due to the inadequacies of the 'state of the art' itself and, more particularly, to the shortcomings of democratic theory which has not yet come to grips with the task of reconciling the demands of democracy with the specific circumstances of heterogeneous societies. Furthermore it is still, almost exclusively, state-centred. It seems to be high time for it to shift its focus from the (allegedly) socio-culturally homogeneous nation-state to the amorphous, socio-culturally heterogeneous supranational quasi-polities. Their decisions unfortunately have increasingly 'direct effect' on the peoples of the various sub-polities. With Robert A. Dahl (1989, p. 2, 311ff.) one might say: it is high time for the 'third transformation' of democracy (and democratic theory), in order to adapt democracy to the new needs evolving in an age of globalisation. Concentrating stubbornly on the nation-state will inevitably lead to 'democratic deficits', not only in the supranational context but also at the national level, because of the ever-widening deviation from the principle of congruence. Now already the set of decision-makers nominally accountable to citizens accounts for a decreasing amount of the decisions to which citizens are actually subjected (see Held 1991). Yet the transfer of the representative institutions commonly expected to guarantee public accountability to higher (supranational) levels does not solve this problem for a variety of reasons, most of which have been discussed above. Instead, it looks as though democratic theory would have to start anew, in a way, by raising age-old basic questions again – namely, 'who is the demos?' (and how does one deal with one that is radically heterogeneous?), 'what is the polity?' (and which elements must be given in order to identify one that can be 'democratised'?), 'which form of democracy?' (and which for which type of polity?) and 'democracy over what?' (and with what limits?).[1]

Not all of these questions will be fully addressed here. Others will be added – mainly that of how to deal (in the above-named context) with sectoral groups, and how to treat wholly informal policy making arrangements. With respect to this ensemble of questions various strands of political and democratic theory will be discussed in a somewhat eclectic manner. I want to find out – from contract theory, the theory of fiscal federalism, theories of group representation, network analysis and game theory, and recent normative ('reflexive') democratic theory – whether they can give hints or even provide usable devices for the democratisation of the European policy making system: whether any plausible alternatives to parliamentarisation and majoritarian democracy exist; whether it is theoretically possible to devise a stable, 'optimal' allocation of powers between various levels of jurisdiction; whether sectoral groupings can be conceptualised as

---

1 For the original questions see Weiler et al. 1995, p. 5.

'demoi' in their own right; whether bargaining systems or networks can be democratised at all. This targeted approach at the same time implies that these theories will be rather cursorily sketched. After a brief look at the essence of the respective theory, I shall proceed to discuss just those elements which touch on my own object.

Contract Theory

Basic Principles

The very theoretical basis of democracy is contract theory, although the first philosopher explicitly to base the 'institutional state' on the notion of an initial 'social contract' was Thomas Hobbes who least of all intended to design a democratic system. At that time, however, the figure of the initial contract *which all individuals* (in the respective society) *have consented to* seemed both necessary and plausible to let the 'rule of man over man' appear legitimate, whether it took democratic shape or not. The general idea was as follows: seeking to gain security, individuals step out of a natural or primordial state in which they used to enjoy unlimited freedom to do what they liked, and renounce their freedom by way of a mutual contract. The consequence of this contract is the formation of a society bound together (and 'civilised') by law, topped by a state as the agency which is to guarantee that the laws are obeyed. In the wake of Hobbes, other authors – John Locke, Immanuel Kant and Jean-Jacques Rousseau in particular – enlarged upon the theme, adding the significant qualification that, if individuals are to consent *voluntarily* to such a contract, the latter must possess certain indispensable features: it must respect basic 'natural rights' (which, with Locke, are almost exclusively property rights), and/or it must provide for procedures to safeguard that these rights will not be violated.[2]

This is not the place to give a detailed account of all the ramifications of classical contract theory which vary according to the authors' notions of human nature, to the conceived natural state, and to the – more or less political – objectives pursued. Suffice it here to state their essence since John Locke: (1) that

2 According to Hobbes, the individual is ready to renounce his right of self-determination whenever all other individuals will do the same (*Leviathan* 1651, XII).

there is no legitimate government without the consent of those governed; (2) that no political order can be judged to be a 'good' (or legitimate) order if it cannot be conceptualised as founded by way of an initial contract between all citizens; (3) that such an order (i.e., the content of the contract) is necessarily 'good' and just because all parties to the contract are endowed with reason and take care not to impose on others what they do not want to have imposed upon themselves (Kant) – or because they all operate under a 'veil of ignorance' (Rawls 1971), meaning that even the most self-interested individual will favour an order that benefits everyone as long as he does not know his own future situation (i.e., does not know beforehand whether or not he might profit from a specific set of rules, disadvantageous to some others).

The bulk of contract theory deals with this last aspect. Aiming at a specific sort of good and just order, it concentrates on the question of how individuals might be trusted (or induced) to bring it about, and why they should do so. The question, however, has never been conceptualised as an empirical one. In all these theories it is not meant to be put to the test; nor do they pretend to refer to historical realities. Both the much talked-about natural state and the initial (or original) contract are purely fictitious, or hypothetical. This limits the practical relevance of classical contract theory considerably. Its main use – or so it seems – would be to provide a model for the justification of political institutions, and a highly ambivalent one into the bargain: it does not ask whether the people did and do consent to an existing institutional set-up but merely whether it is shaped in a way that people *might* have consented, assuming they had been 'reasonable' (which, in its turn, can mean a host of things, the foremost of them being that they are 'disinterested'). Since the notions both of what 'reasonable persons' are, and what they might reasonably consent to, can vary widely, a respectively wide range of political institutions can be classified as legitimate by this device.

Not altogether different from the use that can be made of the construct of the hypothetical contract is that of the 'implicit' contract (Ballestrem 1986) although it is allegedly closer to reality. It does not take a fictitious natural state (or 'original situation', see Rawls 1971) as a starting point but proceeds from a more real-life notion of contract to deduce from this the necessity of a sort of everyday (albeit tacit) consent as the criterion of a legitimate political order. There is no need to renew this consent periodically, or at crucial points of policy making (like, say, major redistributive decisions, or other decisions bordering on constitutional questions) as long as citizens have the possibility both of 'exit' and of 'voice' (Hirschman 1970), that is, as long as neither the voicing of opposition nor emigration are prohibited. 'In order to prove that somebody is a voluntary member [of an organisation, or a community, H.A.] and therefore has voluntarily accepted the members' duties, the decisive point is the possibility of leaving, or of terminating the contract. Whoever does not leave, although he could do so, obviously wants to remain a member.' (ibid. p. 43; translation H.A.).

This maxim of 'silence and cooperation' (or of 'significant silence'; p. 39ff.) very much resembles the 'permissive consensus', said to have supported European integration so far. Both profess to be based on the empirical insight that people generally do not want to be bothered with the 'great political questions'. This fact is open to interpretation, though: it can either mean (1) that people 'break their silence' on petty matters of day-to-day (interest) politics rather than on more fundamental matters;[3] or (2) that people break their silence only when grievance over the political order has crossed a very high threshold indeed. In the second case their 'tacit consent' may in fact cover a considerable amount of discontent. The conclusions to be drawn from this linkage of normative theory and empirical arguments are somewhat disconcerting as regards legitimacy: If voiced opposition can be easily dismissed as petty (and as coming from mere minorities, into the bargain), the actual gain from people's silence looks very much like a conjuring trick. Or, in other words, a semblance of legitimacy is too cheaply won.

Majority Rule or Unanimity?

One may conclude from this brief recital that little use can be made of contract theory in constitutional and legitimatory matters. According to a commentator, the notion of the social contract presents itself as a mere 'intellectual crutch', useful only to get 'a clearer view on the conditions of an inter-individually consensual justification of the principles of social life' (Koller 1986, p. 30; transl. H.A.). There is, however, another aspect of contract theory which may be of greater practical interest. The hypothetical initial contract may serve to determine legitimate rules of decision. Most of the early contractarians have argued that, once the initial

---

3 In fact, the only Bavarian revolution that has ever taken place is said to have happened because of a rise in beer prices.

contract has been agreed upon unanimously (though not all of them are very explicit on this point[4]), subsequent political decisions within the agreed polity are to be taken by simple majority.[5] The justification of majority rule is based, with variations, explicitly or implicitly, (1) on just this previous consent to the initial contract which will contain not only the decision-making rules themselves but also certain limits on the decisions to be taken by majorities (so that individuals can be assured that their human rights and core interests will not be infringed; or else they would have withheld their consent);[6] (2) on general expediency; and (3) on the logical argument that – as all 'reasonable' individuals know (and as Condorcet has proved) – majority rule is the only rule which gives no unfair advantage to anyone. Any quorum bigger than simple majority would allow some minority to outvote the majority; hence simple majority is the rule to minimise the number of those whose wishes are thwarted.

Condorcet notwithstanding, certain conditions will have to be met for majority rule to be acceptable – regarding the amount of shared values (which refers to the homogeneity of the people) and both the reasonableness and the disinterestedness of the parties to the contract who are subsequently individually subjected to majority decisions, not to mention conditions regarding type and effect of decisions. According to Rousseau the main qualification, however, is that the will of the majority be endowed with 'all the characteristics of the general will'; otherwise there will be 'no freedom' under majority rule (book 4, chapter 2). This is why he was not too sure about the general applicability of majority rule and rather wondered whether it might not be a better idea to differentiate decision rules according to the conditions and needs of the 'body politic', and to get the closer to unanimity 'the more important and serious the deliberations' are (ibid.). At any rate he was convinced that the 'general will' had a much fairer chance to dominate the greater the consensus among the people, even though the 'general will' ('volonté générale') was, in his eyes, by no means identical with the 'will of all' ('volonté de tous') but instead the will that 'reason' would have dictated.

While majority rule is indisputably superior to any other decision-making rule (short of the autocratic one) as regards

---

4 But see Rousseau's Contrat Social (1762), book 4, chapter 2.
5 See, for instance, John Locke: *Two Treatises of Government* (1689), VIII, pts. 95ff.
6 Ibid., XI, pts. 134ff.

expediency, political philosophers and liberal philosophers in particular have always felt that it was tainted by some normative shortcomings. Starting from the proposition 'that each [person, H.A.] is the only safe guardian of his own rights and interests',[7] majority rule cannot be 'entirely satisfactory' (Dahl 1989, p. 135). A more recent strand of contract theory, in the shape of 'constitutional economics' based on rigorous methodological individualism and concentrating on the question of decision-making rules and the 'calculus of consent' (Buchanan & Tullock 1962), has come to the conclusion that far from guaranteeing optimality, majority rule is highly problematic and unanimity the only rule which does not pose any normative problems. Any deviation from unanimity rule therefore requires careful and well-founded justification (ibid., pp. 81, 96).

Being contractarian, constitutional economics cannot, of course, do without any concept of a natural, anarchical state. According to Buchanan (1975), the way from this original situation to the institutionalised and active state is rather long and marked by various contracts at different stages of development. Both the rules governing these contracts and the resulting features of the state are essentially shaped by the self-interest, the rationality and especially by the inequality of individuals in their anarchical state. This means that at the early stages of the 'disarmament agreement' and the 'enforcement contract' no 'good' and just order is to be expected: since unanimity is required, those who have been better off before will profit from the new situation, too. In particular, they will consent to an institutionalised state only if this is restricted to a 'neutral' or 'protective' agency, reduced to the enforcement of the contractual terms (ibid., p. 66ff.). Since the state then is solely an agent of jurisdiction and norm application, society at this stage gets along without any political decision-making processes; hence no decision-making rules are needed other than unanimity in case the contract partners should think any revisions of their contract necessary. Problems of collective decision-making arise at the moment when contract partners feel that 'public goods' are needed. Because of the well-known free-rider problem these will have to be provided by an 'enforcing agency', i.e., by the state. The step from the 'protective' to the 'productive state' is again done by contracts: this time 'post-constitutional contracts' which are very difficult to achieve since they cannot and will not be

---

7   J. S. Mill: *Considerations on Representative Government* (1861), chapter III.

agreed upon unanimously. While the free-rider problem will in fact be solved by transferring the production and supply of public goods to the state, this simple transfer would not solve the problems resulting from the basic inequality of individuals. Individuals will be either in need of these goods but unable to pay for them, or the reverse, which inevitably renders the supply of public goods a matter of redistribution.

At this stage, that is, the need for decision-making rules *other* than unanimity makes itself felt, and this is where the 'calculus of consent' comes in. Every non-unanimous decision produces external effects for those individuals who have been outvoted (and to whom one may well believe the respective decision to be detrimental). On the other hand, there are the costs of lengthy decision-making processes to be considered, as well as those accruing when no decision is reached at all (the 'default situation'). So every individual will try, for himself, to minimise the sum of both sorts of costs: external (or frustration) costs and decision-making (or transaction) costs (Buchanan & Tullock 1962, p. 63ff.). The sum will vary with the type of decisions. In the case of interference with 'human or property rights' (p. 73), individuals will seek to avoid high external costs and tend to accept higher decision-making costs than in the case of routine government activity. But the sum will also vary between societies, depending on the degree of inequality or of heterogeneity of values and interests of their members. The 'veil of ignorance' does not always have its beneficial effect; it has 'little relevance for a society that is characterised by a sharp cleavage of the population into distinguishable social classes or separate racial, religious, or ethnic groupings' (p. 80). The situation in such cases will resemble that in the assumed anarchical state: the privileged group(s) will have little incentive to decide in a way paying respect to the rights and interests of other groups as well. Although such reasoning would make a logical case for majority rule for any decision of a redistributive nature (provided the group of the better-off is in the minority), it will not gain acceptance.[8]

In sum, the best decision-making rule, in the normative and strictly individualistic view of libertarians – and the only one to lead to 'optimal decisions by the Pareto criterion' (p. 95) – is unanimity.

8   Although Brennan & Buchanan (1985) explicitly discuss the point, they nonetheless conclude that it is 'at best equivocal' whether or not majority rule will in fact secure 'distributive justice', and that it would be at any rate 'a highly imperfect means' of pursuing this object (pp. 129, 132).

Any deviations from this rule 'will be rationally chosen, not because they will produce 'better' collective decisions (they will not), but rather because, on balance, the sheer costs involved in reaching decisions unanimously dictate some departure from the 'ideal' rule.' (p. 96) Rational behaviour assumed, it is the less likely that such departures will be chosen the more heterogeneous the society is – provided all groups of the society have, in fact, a say in the matter.

Lessons from Contract Theory

At first sight, this brief excursion into the realm of contract theory appears to be rather irrelevant for the decision-making in the EU, which is still mainly a process between nation-state governments. European institutional arrangements so far result from their negotiations. It is difficult to imagine how to apply to them the idea that political institutions are legitimate only in so far as one may safely assume that all *individuals* subjected to them would have consented to them voluntarily. On the other hand, the deduction of specific decision-making rules from a contract model for those governments themselves must look trivial for they are parties to a contract in actual fact – entering contracts voluntarily and, in behaving quite rationally, trading their consent for the highest possible gain.

Yet the legal fact that European norms have 'direct effect' on all citizens justifies a second look which will reveal that some lessons are to be learnt from contractarians, after all – even if they are negative. They can be summarised as follows: (1) the European 'political order' *cannot* be legitimised by way of conclusions drawn from a hypothetical initial contract because the EU is a political entity 'in flux' and not a state. If the figure of contract is to be used at all, it is to be conceptualised not as *one* initial contract but as *iterated* contracts, or a sort of 'initial contract in permanence'. Hence, as yet there can be no contractarian justification for a differentiation of decision-making rules into those for the original contract and those for post-constitutional contracts. (2) Accordingly, some sort of 'permanent consent' is required for the legitimisation of European politics. A conceptualisation of such permanent consent along the lines of the 'implicit contract' (Ballestrem), however, will not suffice, for in a supranational context the individual has little chance to effectively voice his opposition, and virtually none to leave. The notion of 'exit' ought to be supplanted, therefore, by effective ways to withhold – or withdraw – consent.[9]

(3) There is a trade-off between participation in actual decisions and the scope of decision-making (as Locke already indicated): voluntary consent for decision-making rules below unanimity can be construed the more easily the less decisions interfere with individuals, i.e., the less active the polity is going to be. (4) Such voluntary consent can be assumed the less the greater the inequality between the imagined parties to the contract and the more marked the heterogeneity of the society. But we are left with a thorny problem there: beyond a certain threshold of inequality in the 'original', pre-constitutional situation, unanimous consent cannot be seriously supposed, even hypothetically. Would-be partners could not agree on any sort of 'good order', not least because the assumption of the beneficial effect of the veil of ignorance (or of uncertainty[10]) does not hold. Yet on the other hand, it is particularly difficult to imagine consent to any decision-making rule *other* than unanimity in such a case. At the same time, the specific condition of great heterogeneity leads us, once more, to the conclusion that in such a context *no* institutional setting can safely be interpreted in a way so as to comply with the 'as if' rule: i.e., to be legitimate *as if* it had emerged contractually. There is nothing else but to legitimise the respective institutions by actual consent.

Fiscal Federalism

Basic Principles

A federation might be said to be the prime example of a state formed out of heterogeneous components by means of an actual 'initial contract' – entered into, however, by territorial governments who act vicariously and (historically) may or may not have been backed by the consent of their citizens. The traditional theory of federalism, at any rate, (which in this respect includes modern authors like William Riker) has busied itself with questions of governmental behaviour and strategies, or intergovernmental

9 Buchanan, however, in his reflections on 'Europe's Constitutional Opportunity' (1990) envisages exactly the maintenance of the exit option as an essential of any constitutional agreement on a 'federal union' of Europe. He insists on 'the rights of citizens in the separate units to secede from the union', if some 'supra-majority' in the seceding unit takes this decision (p. 7).

10 For the difference between the two see Brennan & Buchanan 1985, p. 29ff.

conflicts, or magical matters such as divided sovereignty, rather than with the consent of subjects or other legitimatory problems. This in part explains, why theorists of democracy tend to argue that federalism and democracy are not wholly compatible since a national majority cannot overrule certain minorities.[11] No matter how great the support it has won in elections, its political agenda is restricted (see Dahl 1983).

The theory of fiscal federalism – one of the strands of institutional (or constitutional) economics and hence equally based on methodologial individualism – avoids the 'top-down' view and the governmental perspective of traditionalist federalist theory and attempts to demonstrate that both democracy and federalism have the same roots in contractualism. According to this theory, federalism is not even exclusively linked to the type of state called 'federation' but is a specific way of territorially allocating the production of public goods[12] which may occur in various types of states or polities. 'In economic terms, all governmental systems are more or less federal' for 'a considerable extent of de facto fiscal discretion at decentralized levels' (Oates 1977, p. 4) exists everywhere. The main idea is that the production of collective goods ought to respond to individual preferences as closely as possible. Since 'man is a territorial animal' (Duchacek 1970, p. 1), it can be safely assumed that in the case of quite a number of those goods preferences are locally or regionally very much alike. Hence the claim that decisions concerning public goods are to be taken at that level of government where in all probability (near-) unanimity can be reached about them. Ideally and in economic terms this stipulation should be identical with the demand of greatest possible congruence between those who decide on, those who pay for, and those who benefit from a public good. External costs and effects are minimised this way, and everybody would be content.

In an ideal world, this principle leads to a plausible and clear-cut distribution of tasks (and, hence, competences) between different levels of government. People might unanimously judge it sensible that the top level – the federal state – provides for security

11 The verdict of incompatibility is the more justified, of course, when (as is the case in Germany) the territorial minorities are represented at the federal level by their governments only.

12 In economic terms, public or collective goods are goods from which many or all citizens of a community benefit, from the benefit of which it is difficult to exclude anyone, and the costs of which are difficult of allocate individually. In political terms, these are all goods which are provided by 'the public' and which are tax-financed. The principles of fiscal federalism may be applied to both types.

and defence, and widely agree on the way it should do so. At the same time they might fundamentally differ in their views about the schooling of children and the role religion is to play in school; in that case it would be very unwise to locate educational policy at the top level which decides for the country as a whole. Doing so would produce suboptimal results and high external costs (not to mention great frustration), and would moreover give rise to unnecessary political conflict. It would be much better to place it at the regional level, provided people agree on the issue regionally. There are, of course, issues on which agreement can at best be reached locally; these should be settled at the municipal level. Where there is no agreement at all, there would be no other choice than to deal with the matter 'privately'.

The principle reads simpler and more plausible than it really is. In the first place it can only be trusted to lead to optimal results when neither 'spill-overs' (meaning that no other units than those which decide benefit or suffer from the decision), nor economies of scale and the like exist. This qualification seriously restricts the number of policy matters to which the principle can be applied for spill-overs occur as soon as you build a road, a chemical plant, canalise a river in your region, and so on: your neighbouring unit(s) would in any such case get to feel the effects of the decision, and mostly in a negative way. At the same time, a lot of public goods people might wish for would never be supplied because the local or regional unit could not afford it. This leads us to the second major qualification: The maxim that matters should be decided upon at the very level at which the respective preferences are homogeneous can only be applied to a certain type of policies. It may be useful when 'allocative' policies are concerned, i.e., the supply of public goods and services. It is, however, not to be used whenever the issues are about redistribution (for there will never be unanimity on this point, not even on a local level); nor is it of any use in matters of economic stabilisation. Thus the range of policies (and competences) which might be fairly distributed between different levels of government is further, and considerably, reduced.

Federalist Ambiguities

In effect, the theory of fiscal federalism can easily be read in two ways: advocating decentralisation and advocating centralisation. The economic reasoning usually starts with the benefits of decentralisation (because it 'improves resource allocation in the public sector through the diversification of public outputs in accordance with local tastes', Oates 1977, p. 9) but ends up with conclusions in favour of centralisation – not least because of the problem of 'horizontal equity' (meaning, economically speaking, that cost-benefit relations are equal in all regions of the country). If it is claimed in the name of the latter that for reasons of fairness and justice taxes should be raised by the central state, then the whole theoretical edifice is seriously marred for then the postulated congruence of deciding over a collective good, profiting from it and paying for it can at best be nominally achieved.[13] Little remains to justify decentralisation if one thinks of the 'organisation costs' (Breton & Scott 1978, chapter 7) accruing from regional elections and administration as well as from inter-regional negotiations which aim at the minimisation of spill-overs. Of course, those costs have to be balanced, in their turn, with the 'preference' or 'frustration costs' which rise considerably with increasing centralisation – provided preferences do indeed vary regionally. To the degree that there is good reason to doubt just this, 'fiscal federalisation', or decentralisation, would not only lose the last of its economic advantages but also its legitimacy.

An economic answer to the latter problem is the argument of 'voting by feet': assuming that the citizens are sufficiently mobile, the competitiveness of fiscal federalism will act as a kind of 'invisible hand' and induce the local/regional units to supply a range of goods and services which is optimally adjusted to *all* citizens' preferences. Yet this argument finds little favour with critics, even under the somewhat unrealistic assumption that people are indeed mobile. For before the happy end-state is reached, the 'voting by feet' could well result in a 'segregation by income' (Oates 1977, p. 7f.) – to a sharp differentiation between rich and poor units – with highly detrimental effects both economically and socially.

Another problem arises when the theorems of fiscal federalism are taken literally: they might then lead to an instrumentalisation of the territorial subdivision of societies. Any 'given' regional/local unit, as well as the number of levels of government, are

13 The problem could be solved by 'block grants', of course (i.e., by subsidies of the federal government to lower units which are not included into any specific policy programme or in any other way dedicated to a specific purpose). But there remains a basic dependence of lower units on the top level which will affect their autonomy of decision.

(theoretically) 'at disposal' at any given time, to be altered according to changes in the people's preferences concerning collective goods or other aspects of governance. As Robert A. Dahl lets his federalist 'James' argue (against 'Jean-Jacques'), 'we can't assume that a single aggregate of persons would be best served by only one system. Garbage removal, water supply, schools, pollution, defense – each of these might produce a different optimum. The result might well be a complex system with several or many layers of democratic government, each operating with a somewhat different agenda' (Dahl 1989, p. 205). What's more, these layers, and the boundaries between them, would be constantly in a state of flux. We would end up with a highly unstable ensemble, hardly compatible with our customary image of a 'state'; and political scientists would immediately lament its 'ungovernability'.[14] Even economists have some doubts about federalist models resting solely on aspects of allocative efficiency. Thus Peter Bohley (1994, p. 546ff.) attempts to complement the theory of fiscal federalism with an institutionalist approach which attributes a specific benefit (named 'immediate citizen's benefit') to the institutions of the regional or local unit the individual belongs to and to the sense of regional 'identity' he derives from this 'belonging'. While it seems highly plausible to attach an own value to territorial institutions, traditions and identities, the additional (economic) benefit deduced from them, however, damages the theory's stringency in so far as it renders its reasoning in tendency tautological. Any given federalist structure can this way be proved to be efficient simply by putting a respectively high value on the 'citizen's benefit'.

Other aspects of the fiscal-federalist perspective stress more practical and government-oriented principles, such as 'fair burden-sharing' (between citizens in the various territorial 'servicing areas') or 'fiscal equalisation' (between richer and poorer units, and between regional and top levels). Together with the principles of 'optimal assignment' and 'optimal differentiation of competences', of 'correspondence' (or congruence, see above), and of subsidiarity (see Hesse & Wright 1996, p. 107ff.) they form the model which is currently, rather undisputedly, taken as a guiding line for the way federalist systems ought to operate, providing criteria by which their performance is to be judged. Applied to the

---

14 Not all of them, however. In Germany some political scientists belong to the most ardent advocates of a fundamental restructuring of the territorial division into *Länder*, following the maxims of fiscal efficiency.

EU, these criteria (as we have already seen above) result in the assessment that it is 'not yet' a federation and 'beyond' federalism at the same time. The lack of an autonomous tax authority (which violates the 'correspondence principle'; ibid., p. 112) certainly places it on the 'not yet' side; the way competences are transferred to the top level (which violates the subsidiarity principle) on the side of 'beyond'. The principles of 'optimal assignment' and 'optimal differentiation' of competences also seem to be violated, and rather conspicuously at that. Surprisingly enough, economists do not altogether agree on which side the error lies in this matter, some of them deploring a sad 'under-utilisation of the EU decision-making capacity' (ibid.), while others criticize the unwarranted expansion of top-level competences.

Lessons from Fiscal Federalism

This indicates that the lessons to be learnt from the theory of fiscal federalism are much less straightforward than might have been expected. In fact, I must offer my apologies to authors of reform proposals concentrating on federalist matters for criticising them as being too vague. (1) The first lesson is that, unfortunately, criteria for the allocation of competences at different levels of government are far from theoretically clear-cut, and hence of little use in practice. Consequently, any 'catalogue of competences' must be theoretically unsatisfactory and practically deficient, even if it is based on sound empirical data about people's preferences. If this is so, the only possible federalist conclusion is to keep any distribution of competences *flexible*. Enumerative catalogues may be helpful because they can put brakes on the trend to further centralisation but there is probably little sense in fixing them once and for all. Instead, it seems sensible to make it possible that any given distribution – especially any transfer of powers to the top layer – is revocated by the lower levels. In the terms of fiscal federalism, powers should be handed back to lower levels if agreement on the respective matters proves (after all) to be greater at this than at top level.[15]

(2) The theory does *not* allow a definite conclusion concerning the *scope* of top level competences: how narrowly or generously they are to be circumscribed. There is nothing but the subsidiarity principle to caution us not to deprive the lower levels of essential powers. One

---

15 See the respective proposal of the ECG (1993, 'Draft Statement', p. 10).

may, however, generally conclude (as I have already done from contract theory) that specific attention has to be paid to the factor of heterogeneity. For the more heterogeneous the component units of a federation are, the more a concentration of decision-making powers at the federal (or top) level will lead to suboptimal results, regardless of the 'system capacity' and the prima facie decision-making efficiency of this level. Performance will always be marred by the high 'frustration costs' incurred by citizens of the component units. Once more, this same conclusion leads to the other that it is mostly unwise from a theoretical point of view for a union of heterogeneous parts to follow the model of the 'active state'.

(3) Most of the practical conclusions that can be drawn from the theory regard finances and will not be discussed here since my main concern is about matters of legitimacy. But one further aspect ought at least to be mentioned: the 'segregation by income' (Oates 1972, 1977). Too much autonomy – or deficits in (top-down) harmonisation – might induce migration processes to the 'better-off' units (i.e., those with the better social and employment policy, the higher standards of environment protection, etc., not to mention a generally higher standard of living). Some decades ago one would have argued, rather confidently, that this particular 'voting by feet' was of limited practical relevance, considering the great cultural heterogeneity of the citizens of member countries as well as their sense of 'national identity'. In the 1990s, however, and with the effects of cultural globalisation, one can be much less certain about this. So here might be an argument in favour of central (or federal) regulation and harmonisation.

Concepts of Group Representation

Modern societies are not only territorially divided. Within territories as well as across their boundaries groups are (quasi-) united by common features of their 'objective' (socio-economic) situation, hence – as one should expect – by common interests. But it has always been a problem for social theory to determine how such 'potential groups' (Bentley 1908) are transformed into 'manifest groups', what sort and intensity of 'collective identity' and which other prerequisites have to be given. An additional question comes to the fore in our present context. One of the major difficulties (if not to say dilemmas) of democratic theory is how to draw the proper boundaries (see Whelan 1983): how are the *demoi* of self-governing units to be identified, who is to be included and who to be excluded in a democratic policy-making system – and who is to decide upon the matter? Where the territorial dimension of politics is concerned (and where history helps to facilitate matters), it seems to be comparatively easy to establish who belongs and who does not. But assuming that there exists a sectoral (or functional) dimension of politics and (possibly) of democratic self-government besides the territorial dimension, we immediately get into trouble when we try to find answers to the tricky question of who is to participate and who not.

Most of the theories dealing with group representation do not even make the attempt to answer this fundamental question. Pluralists, in particular, have long since discovered the 'group basis of politics' (Latham 1965) but bothered little about what it was that transformed individuals who did not even know each other into a group; the existence of sectoral groups was taken more or less for granted. It was of course recognised that it took some steps before a 'quasi group' of individuals in structurally similar or equal situations became conscious of their common 'latent' interests and gradually grew into an 'actual' group (or association) with 'manifest' interests and a 'visible identity of its own' (Dahrendorf 1962, p. 218ff.). But how the establishment of such an identity would reveal itself seemed so simple that no debate seemed necessary: it was unquestionably given when people organised themselves. And for them doing just this, little was needed beyond the common 'latent interests': it took some serious threat (of whichever sort) and some activists. The latter were thought to turn up rather automatically, as (for instance) in the theorem of 'countervailing powers' (Galbraith 1952). They would emerge when needed – in this case, at the moment when rivalling interests had organised and threatened to become so powerful as to thwart one's own interests. Once organised, it was easy to identify those who belonged – they were those who paid the fees, joined strikes and other actions, and/or voted for the political parties affiliated with or allied to the respective associations.

Pluralists felt no need to delve deeper into matters of boundary and collective identity because the question of legitimate decision-making by group representatives did not crop up in their theories. Group leaders would act on behalf of group members, and of group members alone. They would be prevented (a) from taking it upon themselves to unrightfully act for others, or even for the whole community, (b) from digressing too far from members' interests while pursuing their own self-interest, and (c) from doing harm to the common good, all by one device: by the 'invisible hand' of group competition (of which the quasi-automatic emergence of 'countervailing powers' only formed a part). Like the associations themselves, the common good would 'emerge': The result of the competition between all the organised interests, or the 'resultant ... from the parallelogramm of economic, social, political and ideological forces' (Fraenkel 1964, p. 21; transl. H.A.) could not be anything else than the optimum welfare of all those concerned, and in pluralist theory the general welfare is not to be determined otherwise.

Guild Socialism

Other concepts building upon (organised) groups as the main political actors could get around boundary and legitimacy problems less easily. Once such groups are to partake in the exercise of 'public power', it must be ascertained whom they represent, and whether their political powers are based on identifiable collective entities reaching beyond the comparatively small numbers of organised activists. Guild socialism and neo-corporatism are concepts to be mentioned in this context. Both can be said to be closely related to pluralism, the first as a sort of 'socialist pluralism', the second as a prolongation of pluralism into the age of 'organised capitalism'. Guild socialism may be interpreted as a compromise between socialist (and even anarchist) demands to abolish the (bourgeois) state on the one hand and the more pragmatic notion that it might be unrealistic as well as unwise to expect the state to wither away on the other. Hence the idea to instrumentalise the state as much as possible but to limit its functions strictly and to decentralise them, devolving its powers, however, to functional groups rather than to local communities. 'Thus guild socialism was to ensure a form of second-order autonomy for functional groups within the limits of overall public policy expressed through the collectivist state.' (Barker 1978, p. 99)[16] Although normal parliamentary democracy was on the whole to be preserved, its general primacy in questions of public policy was contested. At least in economic matters, group functions – in particular those of 'producers' – were to gain primacy over those of the state; in practice this should have meant that trade unions (solely or in cooperation with some other organised interests) determine economic and social policies.

16 Barker draws mainly from the writings of G.D.H. Cole.

With G.D.H. Cole's *Social Theory* (1970, first published in 1920), these pragmatic notions were overarched by a theory of an altogether 'functional' political system which builds on the assumptions (1) that individuals with 'common purposes' will organise in (functional) associations; (2) that the state is fit to deal with those matters 'which affect all its members more or less equally and in the same way' but not with those which affect people differently (p. 96ff.); and (3) that 'man' as such (and as a whole) cannot be 'represented', but his various purposes can. Combined, the assumptions lead to the construct of a new, 'true' and 'functional democracy' which grants utmost autonomy to the functional associations and is based on a system of 'functional representation' where representatives 'represent not persons, but definite and particular purposes common to a number of persons' (p. 106), and according to which any individual with several strong interests will possess several votes, too (p. 115). At the top the whole system was, if necessary, to be coordinated by a kind of 'joint council' of associations.[17]

Neo-Corporatism

In essence, the neo-corporatist approach resembles the guild socialist one, only omitting the socialist element. The notion of 'producers' powers', which must be read as trade union powers, is thus transformed into that of the 'tripartist arrangement' based on the parity of class associations. Like guild socialism (as well as the various strands of federalism), neo-corporatism combines the principle of group autonomy ('leave us alone') with that of the groups' (proportional) participation in public policy making ('let us in'). In a similar way it claims that where matters of economic and social policies are concerned, priority ought to be given to the 'expert' opinion of the associations of business and labour and their decisions take precedence over those of parliaments and their majorities. In both theories, that is, we find the same implicit or

---

17 This, however, was to be shaped after the model of a 'Supreme Court of Functional Equity' rather than of a vocational or economic Second Chamber. In later years Cole tended to be sceptical about the possibility of making any of such institutions influential. 'In a differently ordered society, it might be desirable to create, as a measure of functional devolution, some sort of separate Economic Parliament. But no such institution is likely to work well under capitalism'; hence hoping to resolve the antagonism of capital and labour 'by establishing an Economic Parliament under the existing system is sheer illusion.' (1938, p. 45)

explicit tendency to juxtapose two arenas in which decisions for the society as a whole are taken, and a similar ambivalence about the question which of them is to have the 'last word', and how such privileges are to be justified. Cole, for one, would have argued that 'functional representation' is intrinsically more democratic than the 'normal' one because the former allows for a higher degree of accountability: their specific interest and greater closeness renders group members more fit than voters to control their representatives (1970, p. 109f.). Other authors prefer to ignore the question of how the corporatist or group arena might be legitimised, in case the final decisions actually reside in the latter instead of in the parliamentary arena where, traditionally, public accountability is supposed to rest.

On the whole, both theories have rather neglected the question of how to legitimise 'public' decision-making by groups. Even more remarkable is that they have spent little thought on criteria to distinguish the groups. Like normal pluralists, they took organised groups, their existence and their emergence out of somewhat broader reference groups, for granted. In their eyes no obstacle apart from their own disinterest would hinder individuals with 'common purposes' to associate, seeking to pursue these purposes by cooperation. In part, there is even an authoritarian touch to the notion of group, in so far as the one (guild socialism) is based on the analogy to medieval guilds into which members were born, while in the other those associations best suited to corporatist arrangements are likened to cartels or monopolies into which members are forced (see Schmitter & Lehmbruch 1979, p. 20f.). Visualising group membership as compulsory renders the boundary question indeed pointless, but leaves that of the proper legitimisation unanswered.

The Recipes of Social Theory

It is difficult to make out sectoral collective identities once one tries to retrace the emergence of the 'end product', the organised group. New approaches dealing with the matter of collective identity busy themselves primarily with those of a territorial nature. 'Cultural identity', for instance, is usually defined in terms of national, ethnic, linguistic homogeneity firmly connected to some territorial (local, regional, national) bases. According to the common argument, identification stops (mysteriously enough) at the national level and does not go beyond this territorial boundary.

This is why common reasoning will have it that it is an exceedingly difficult task to develop a 'European identity'. Identification resting on other – sectoral or functional – bases might, however, easily transcend these borderlines and establish cross-national bonds. Unfortunately, and much to the chagrin of nineteenth-century class theorists, there has as yet been little evidence of 'social identities' actually transcending national ones.

Of course there are (as has been mentioned above) 'objective' criteria of functional and/or sectoral differentiation, set out by social theory – whether class, role or system theory. Marxist class theory, coming closest to a plausible concept of social identity, intends to deduce specific ways of thinking, feeling, forming interests etc. – i.e., 'class interests' as well as a 'class consciousness' – from the individuals' objective position within the production process and the given system of the division of labour. The step from objective class position to subjective class consciousness, however, is more convincingly demonstrated with employers ('capitalists') than with workers. In the case of the former, individual interest (to gain a profit) and class interest (to extract a 'surplus') are compatible if not identical; whereas the individual worker's interest (to get a job and, in order to achieve this, accept a low wage) will tend to run counter to the workers' class interest which is to limit and (in the long run) end exploitation. Workers are led into conflict with fellow workers as well as with their class when they act in line with their subjective interest as an individual. As long as they are taken in by this specific kind of 'veil of ignorance', called 'false consciousness', they can hardly be expected to develop a collective identity which is in accordance with their objective situation. Consequently (and as Marx himself has argued) the precondition of similarity of objective situations does not suffice for the formation of a collective (or social) identity. If their false notions of their own interests are to be overcome, individuals may indeed have to be hard worked upon, and a lot of convincing may have to be done.

Hence the concept of class identity is marked by a certain flavour of artificiality. In contrast to this theoretical conclusion, empirical findings from the last 150 years or so show that workers do tend to develop a strong sense of coherence and solidarity, and an even stronger sense of difference from 'them' at the top. But a closer look invariably reveals (1) that especially the first-mentioned feelings have traditionally been heavily influenced by 'activists', that is, by trade unions and their precursors. In other words: the 'potential group', which is the logical precedent of the actual association, has been created and shaped by the latter to a considerable extent. Another discovery will usually be (2) that the objective (economic) situation, which is the supposed independent variable for the formation of a collective identity, is typically mingled with quite a number of additional variables that are at least as 'independent' as the first: the community spirit derived from living in the same territory, or from working in the same industry, not to mention adherence to the same religion.

Role theory has been another attempt to establish criteria for the development of social identities. Individuals acting in the same role (or social position), or so it is argued, will not only act in similar ways but adopt the same set of values and probably form similar interests. Yet the step from this objective criterion to subjective identification is somewhat less plausible than was the case with that of class. For while belonging to a certain class may well affect a considerable part of one's life, acting in a certain role does concern a smallish sector only since everybody takes on many different roles at the same time. Moreover, acting a social role does not necessarily imply knowing those who act in similar positions and communicating with them; nor does it imply reflecting this position at all (whether in a false way or not). It even seems safe to assume that reflection (as a possible first step to identification) occurs the less the more successful the socialisation into the respective social role has been. Ironically, this might give rise to the notion of a collective identity of maladapters – if some sort of collective identity could be expected to arise from the enactment of roles at all.

In the present context, even less help will come from the quarters of theories of functional differentiation, such as system theory. The theoretical division of a society into various functionally defined subsystems does not lead to any result as regards collective identities, for any individual will, as a rule, belong to several subsystems (political, economic, educational, etc.) at the same time. When system theory does not disregard the individual altogether, it expects him to adapt flexibly to all the different subsystems' norms and 'codes', without thinking much about them. They are not meant to constitute specific loyalties, let alone solidarities; hence neither a 'consciousness' nor a sense of belonging are required of the individual.

Empirical Variants

So in the case of the 'group basis of politics' we end up with the result that social theory contributes but little to the solution of the European problem. Perhaps one then had better take a look at more empirically oriented concepts. To start with, one of the major findings of recent decades has been the discovery of an increasing 'individualisation' of (Western) societies.[18] In a continuous process of 'disembedding' (Giddens 1991), traditional socio-cultural environments ('milieus') dissolve and traditional allegiances vanish (as, in fact, the very 'group basis of politics' would threaten to do, were it not for the comparatively small circles of businessmen and the like, lobbying heavily in order to instrumentalise politics for their ends). As a result, it becomes exceedingly risky to assume certain constants of behaviour still to exist, no matter how much economic and/or social situations seem to call for specific types of behaviour.

As we have just seen, it was always a trifle doubtful to infer specific individual allegiances from an environment defined in terms of social structure. Yet there used to be enough empirical evidence to let one take a high correlation between both for granted. This is one of the reasons why a concept like party identification appeared plausible and for some time proved to be a useful tool to explain and to predict voting behaviour. Somewhat simplified, the reasoning ran as follows:[19] Adherence to social groups (into which individuals in part are literally born) leads voters to identify with those political parties closest to the respective social groups' values. As a consequence, it is to a high degree pre-decided how their votes will be cast in 'normal' cases, i.e., when nothing untoward happens.[20] But nowadays – in the age of individualisation – it is increasingly difficult to determine what such a 'normal vote' would be, albeit not only on the grounds of weakening ties to social groups; the assumed relationship between the said groups and political parties is also called into question. So in the end the concept of party identification boils down to the attempt to establish certain political habits, rather arbitrarily based. The question then remains how often an individual voter must have deviated from his habit to be called a floating voter instead of an 'identifier'.

18 See Giddens 1991; Beck 1993; Berger 1996 for empirical data.
19 See, *inter alia*, Campbell et al. 1966. For a comprehensive discussion of the concept and for comparative empirical data see Budge et al. 1976.
20 For the concept of the 'normal vote' see Converse, especially, in: Campbell et al. 1966, pp. 9-39.

This reads as if electoral researchers were faced with problems quite similar to the search for the possible bases of sectoral groups. There is, however, a decisive difference: apart from pragmatical reasons, electoral researchers do not really need to bother about the social bases of political parties. The existence of socially based party identification might facilitate their work. But it is of little legitimatory relevance if the parties' former bases erode since voters have the chance to decide periodically on decision-makers and correct 'errors' of representation. (Quasi-) members of sectoral groups do not necessarily have this chance – and quite systematically not, as long as one cannot ascertain who is to be included and who not. If the participation of sectoral actors in European decision-making is to be legitimised properly, some sort of representative interrelation is required. To establish this one needs evidence of the existence of respective sectoral entities and a notion about their boundaries. In the national context, the problem does not arise (or at least to a much lesser extent) because the systems of organised interests, of political parties and of government are normally closely connected. In particular, corporatist societies take great care to keep those three levels firmly linked to each other. In the European polity, however, both the party system and the formal government structure are somewhat under-developed; above all, there is neither much interconnection between them nor between both and the budding lobbyist system. Hence, the legitimatory bond arising from the linkage of the 'group politics' arena to the electoral arena is lacking.

How to Identify Sectoral Groups

Unfortunately, when it comes to the question how to bridge this particular legitimatory gap, the various concepts considered here provide little help. Generally, three ways of identifying sectoral groups present themselves: (1) The first is to restrict oneself, conceptually as well as practically, to those who actually organise, assuming that those who do *not* thus have expressed their wish *not* to belong to the respective entity (because of cross-cutting allegiances, preferences of low intensity, or whatever). Although there is at first sight some plausibility in proceeding this way, empirical findings tell us that it is as unjust as the assumption is heroic. Not every 'potential group' has the same chance of organising, and not everybody has the same chance of joining. In particular, there is definitely no evidence that 'countervailing powers' do in fact emerge; hence any given system of organised interests is highly selective as well as skewed.

(2) The second way is to rely on objective criteria such as 'industry' or 'market', combining different views and interests concerning the same subject matter. The flaw in this approach is that there must be considerable doubt about the degree to which people can identify with such sectors, especially since in reality these will inevitably be marked by a high degree of artificiality. As likely as not, the respective boundaries would cut across close economic interrelations; on the other hand, any economic interconnection may be altogether irrelevant for the formation of social identities. In short, sectoral units mapped out in this way are bound to be highly arbitrary.

(3) The third way is simply to ask people about their respective identities. This is the way political allegiances are typically found out. Whether it will lead to likewise convincing results with respect to sectoral identification is doubtful, for while in the first case they are asked about organisations and persons, in the second they would have to be asked both about their stance in sectoral conflicts and about a self-placement within the complex system of society. The tricky problem arising from this is that the self-placement will vary according to matters of dispute. As a result, we would probably be left with a fluid conglomerate of shifting units and not with stable sectoral units which could be inserted into a legitimatory system, one way or the other. The boundaries and the constellations between them would vary both with issues and over time.

In essence, such an approach resembles Whelan's (1983) 'all-affected principle' according to which the proper way to define a participatory unit ought to include all those 'affected by a particular law, policy, or decision' (p. 16). As Whelan argues, this principle 'cannot be implemented in the context of the state' since 'it would require a different constituency of voters or participants for every decision' (p. 18f.). Yet recently Philippe Schmitter (1994) has reminded us of a practical method how just this can be achieved: individuals who either strongly identify with some organised group or feel strongly affected by certain decisions could be equipped with an additional instrument of participation in the shape of (tax-like) vouchers.[21] The vouchers would enable citizens to strengthen the associations of their choice without having to join

---

21 In this concept every citizen would pay the same amount of money into a special fund; and every one would himself determine which association is to receive his contribution. This decision would be renewed periodically.

them, and to further or hinder decisions impacting on their lives and interests more purposefully than is possible by merely voting for a political party. The flaw in this new approach is that it solely rests on organised groups. Since the associations to be thus supported would, in Schmitter's proposal, be endowed with 'semi-public status', the bias would not only be towards organised groups but in addition one towards those which are 'authoritatively recognised'. That is why this scheme can be expected to allow for too little of that flexibility which seems to be required in an age of individualisation and 'disembedding'. Yet the proposal sounds interesting enough to be debated further. It will especially have to be asked whether and how it could be made applicable to the European – non-state – policy arena.

Network Analysis and Game Theory

The European policy arena is marked not only by a plurality of public actors (of different levels) but more particularly by a host of private actors. The number of lobbyists of all sorts in Brussels has exploded in recent years (since the SEA, to be precise). In 1992, the Commission counted approximately 3,000 interest groups of varying kinds (including about 500 European federations of them). You have to add a further 200 representatives of individual firms, about fifty offices representing the *Länder*, regions and local authorities, and about a hundred offices of 'consultants' (Grande 1996b, p. 320). One explanation for the rapid growth of lobbyism in Europe is the growing importance of the European arena. Another is the openness and the high fragmentation of the institutional setting: the great number of lobbyists corresponds with a multiplicity of 'points of access' for their activities. In fact, van Schendelen (1993, p. 11) notices 'not a shortage but an over-supply of potential routes' of influence.

The Analysis of Policy Networks

The normal way of 'private' influence on public policies is that to add informal layers to institutionalised political decision-making in cabinets and parliaments. For some time now it has come to be a habit to depict such informal arrangements as 'policy networks'. 'The term network is on the way to becoming the new paradigm for the "architecture of complexity"' (Kenis & Schneider 1991,

p. 25); the question is whether it is more than a metaphor for complex horizontal interrelations and of more than heuristic value for political analysis.

In political science, policy networks are defined as policy-making arrangements beyond hierarchical and majoritarian decision-making, as well as self-regulatory processes beyond markets. They are informal but comparatively lasting horizontal structures of communication and cooperation, combining a number of public and/or private collective actors (partly even individuals) with stakes in the same sectors, or policy areas. These arrangements are stabilised by the actors' knowledge that they are mutually interdependent, as well as by their common expectations as to behaviour and goal achievement. In essence, the networks are bargaining systems and as such operating on a consensual basis, which distinguishes them from hierarchical and majoritarian modes of decision-making. Consensus, in its turn, is based on exchange – but of either a complex nature (since a network consists, as a rule, of more than just one pair of exchange partners) or even a 'generalized' nature (see Marin 1990). Hence networks do not necessarily operate after the quid pro quo fashion, which distinguishes them from market-like processes.

Analysts may, however, be somewhat led astray when contrasting networks too sharply with the hierarchical system of political institutions. Typically – in nation-states at least – they do not usurp the latter's place but act as an addition (actors from the latter forming 'knots' in the networks themselves), rendering it more flexible and influencing the contents of its decision-making (see Benz 1996, p. 24). The linkage with the political institutions provides the legitimisation of policies (pre-) decided in informal circles of actors normally not entitled to decide for the general public. But the legitimatory 'umbrella' gets the more threadbare the looser this connection is and the more autonomously networks are allowed to act. It may be concluded that policy networks pose some legitimatory problems of their own.

Unfortunately, network analysis as well as theories of bargaining systems tend not to deal with questions of this sort but to concentrate on matters of efficiency,[22] as a closer look will reveal.

---

22 Strictly speaking, sociological network analysis deals with neither of these questions. Instead, its main object is to find out the positions and possible configurations of actors in networks and the patterns of the links between them (including their reciprocity, and the like); see Turner 1991, chapter 27. What I am describing here is the use political scientists make of network analysis.

For this we may well take Fritz Scharpf's (1988) theoretical analysis of the 'joint decision-making' in bargaining systems as a starting point. According to him, joint decision-making will always and necessarily prove inefficient (1) because of its (implicit) unanimity principle which will frequently lead to blockades. These blockades will, in their turn, unduly protect the status quo because of the 'default condition': not coming to an agreement will not normally (as contractarian advocats of unanimity assume) result in the policy matter's remaining unregulated, but will instead prolong existing regulations, no matter how unjust or deficient these regulations are judged by part or even most of the actors forming the bargaining system, nor how intense their wish to have them altered.

(2) In order to overcome such blockades, modes of problem solving will be favoured from which all participants will directly profit. Solutions will be heavily skewed towards subsidies or other forms of pecuniary benefits; hence such systems will be inefficient because they are unduly costly, not to mention the many problems which cannot be adequately solved by payments (and side-payments). (3) A third deficiency results from the fact that participants in bargaining systems are almost exclusively government members, administrators and (group or business) executives. This adds a further bias and high selectivity to the process since these actors will promote the specific 'institutional self-interest' of their respective organisation (or institution), instead of representing societal interests, however narrowly (sectorally) defined.

It is one of the objects of (political) network analysis to prove that these deficiencies are not necessarily in-built but that on the contrary the output of policy networks can be superior to that of hierarchies and markets. For (to start with the latter) actors are assumed not to be isolated *homines oeconomici*, unable to perceive any good beyond their own narrow self-interest. Taking the highly organised modern society with its manifold interdependencies for granted, the actors network analysis reckons with are (1) collective actors, (2) already linked up with others in multiple ways, and hence (3) conscious of a common good only to be achieved by cooperation.[23] The propensity for cooperation which leads participants to join policy networks will be both the more probable and the greater as they can all be certain not to enter a pair-wise exchange situation which in the end might turn out to be one of a

---

23 In this, the analysis draws subcutaneously from oligopoly theory, although the analogy is rarely mentioned.

zero-sum game. Instead they will trust to find themselves placed in a kind of generalised 'exchange chain' from which they may all benefit somehow, especially in the longer run. This reasoning, of course, presupposes that policy networks will usually be permanent.

Whereas the superiority of the policy networks' outcomes over market results is presumed to accrue from their actors' ability to avoid the notorious 'prisoner's dilemma', their superiority over the policy output of hierarchies (i.e., of governments) rests on more pragmatical arguments. In sectorally segmented societies dominated by organised actors, active governments inevitably run into problems with regard to the acquisition of adequate information and to the implementation of their policies. One of the responses to these problems has been the growing decentralisation and fragmentation of the state itself. By this means governments tried to adapt both to the changing structure and the changing needs of society. Such adaption has considerable drawbacks, however: the fragmented governments increasingly lack the ability to coordinate their own policies, not to mention their 'steering' capacity. While the state is thus 'deprived of its mystique' (Willke 1983), policy networks come to its rescue, ensuring that socio-economic developments do not wholly get out of hand. Instead of making them the objects of their regulatory activities, government officials then cooperate with the relevant societal actors, trying to achieve policy results by dint of compromise and exchange. The performance of this kind of 'contextual steering' (ibid.) or 'societal self-regulation' may look somewhat suboptimal and the resulting path of socio-economic development far from straight and smooth. But it seems quite reasonable to go for 'second-best' solutions when optimal solutions are not to be found.

Game Theory as a Helpful Tool

Network analysis itself does not offer much theoretical evidence for this thesis of superior efficiency; nor can it, from the particular constellations in networks, cogently deduce any specific 'logic' of behaviour which would allow predictions. This is why respective authors like to take recourse to game theory. At first sight this might come as a surprise, since game theory – as the theory of strategic decisions – can be regarded as the one to detect (and describe) strategic dilemmas, instead of solving them. Its starting point in analysing the behaviour of actors in networks accordingly is the 'negotiator's dilemma' (Scharpf 1993a, p. 138). For negotiators are as self-interested as any other actor dealt with by rational choice theory. They enter into negotiations because they recognise a common interest and are convinced that a cooperative solution to the problem they are dealing with will be superior to any other solution and make them all better off. Yet self-interested negotiators will, of course, disagree about the details of the solution and will moreover fear that they may be exploited by their partners in the cooperation; hence caution and distrust will generally impair cooperation. In negotiative networks this dilemma can be overcome because they lack a feature that is prominent in situations that resemble the prisoner's dilemma: the uncertainty about the others' intentions, as well as about pay-offs. Since their interrelations in networks are of some duration, negotiators soon learn that it does not pay to harm the others and that, on the contrary, in doing so they run the risk of being excluded from future profitable interactions; 'there is thus a high premium on the capacity for trustworthy communications and commitments among interdependent actors' (ibid., p. 149). Negotiators in networks play 'iterated games' in which they come to know each other and to know the others' intentions. At the same time, the stability and permanence of networks prolongs each actor's time horizon. Gradually they will all form longer-term expectations; the longer the time horizon the more fully they will learn to appreciate the amount of the gains arising from cooperation.

There still remains the problem that actors in networks participate not as individuals but as 'corporate actors' who act in the name of organisations (administrations, governments, etc.). They move in two different circles, act in two different contexts, and have to adapt to two different sets of role expectations; in other words, they have to play a 'two-level game'.[24] The one level is the network and the other their ('home') organisation, and both parts of the game may well be in conflict. Success in one of them can, in some cases, enhance the chance of success in the other, but in other cases it will be just the other way round; in particular it is very likely that the necessities of the 'home game' (the electoral game, for instance) will restrict the scope for manoeuvre and compromise in the negotiative game. Although the permanence as well as the informal character of policy networks may help to facilitate the required tightrope walk of 'double-edged diplomacy', such an effect is by no means guaranteed. On the contrary, it is

---

24 Which, since Putnam (1988), has come to be regarded as a typical feature of international negotiations.

exactly the 'iterated' network games which are apt to prove fatal at the other level, in that they estrange the respective actor from his group or organisation. Above all, neither the actual behaviour nor the outcome are predictable. So in the end we are not much wiser than before. This chastising discovery is, however, not only valid for the behaviour in networks. With the notion of 'nested games' Tsebelis (1990) has shown that any apparently suboptimal – or irrational – behaviour of actors can be explained by their playing a connected (or 'nested') game in another arena, necessitating the deviations from strategies that rational choice theory would have predicted. Once we accept multiple arenas and connected games, behaviour becomes (theoretically) wholly contingent.

Networks and the Problem of Democracy

This obviously is a problem for theories concentrating on the strategies of rational actors. In our context, however, it is anyway not sufficient to deal with strategies. Nor are the probable losses or gains in efficiency our main concern. For the most conspicuous deficit of *real* policy networks is their lack of accountability and democratic control. In this respect, neither (political) network analysis nor game theory prove particularly helpful. Democratic requirements are either ignored or (more or less explicitly) conceived as sources of friction: they crop up in the shape of the – mostly irritating – 'second-level game' or, more plainly, of 'specific impediments to cooperation' (Benz et al. 1992, p. 129). Neither theory reflects that negotiators in bargaining systems are not 'principals' but 'agents', and that provisions are needed to hold the agents responsible to principals if the outcomes of their negotiations are to be considered legitimate and to be acceptable by the principals.

Yet both approaches do seem to provide tools to deal with this matter – or at least hints where these might be sought. Network analysis in its more 'pure' sociological (or even mathematical) versions tries to find out specific and/or typical configurations and constellations – mainly in order to identify the most 'central' actors in a network, assuming (not unjustly) that network interrelations are asymmetrical as a rule and that the more centrally placed actors are the more powerful ones. Modelling such configurations is a first step in dealing with the problem of democracy. A second step would be to model likewise the interactive processes within networks, with the object of depicting likely 'intervention points' at which controls or correcting interventions on the part of reference groups might be sensible and feasible. Game theory hints in a similar (indirect) way at the possibility to link *systematically* the game in the 'principal arena' (i.e., the network, or bargaining system) with the 'home arena', with the same object of allowing for corrections deemed indispensable by reference groups.

Primarily concerned with outcomes and efficiency, most analysts of policy networks would rather not follow such paths. While (in part, at least) acknowledging the legitimatory deficits of bargaining systems, they advise alternative remedies, such as the close and obligatory linking of policy networks to the institutions of the political system (which then have to rubber-stamp the compromises reached by the former's negotiations). A gradual change of group members' attitudes, a recognition that members of opposite groups are partners rather than adversaries – thus another suggestion – may help a lot to defuse the legitimatory problem (see Scharpf 1993b, p. 43f.). Some authors do not take this problem over-seriously anyway because of the networks' openness: principally any group that is 'affected' by a certain policy may participate in the respective network. However, that is exactly what is in doubt in political reality. A symmetrical participation in policy networks of all those affected is as unlikely as is the automatic emergence of 'countervailing powers' (see above); the various 'points of access' are not equally open (nor even known) to every group. Policy networks may in fact reduce the 'structural selectivity' of the formally institutionalised decision-making system for they are informal and concentrate on specific issues rather than on bureaucratic and/or procedural routines. On the other hand, they nonetheless generate a specific selectivity of their own which will be higher or lower depending on the extent to which the associations acting in the respective policy area form cartels or are monopolies. Consequently, selectivity can be expected to be exceedingly high in the field of agricultural policy, for instance, which in many countries is governed by one monopolistic organisation. But even where selectivity is low some doubt may still exist about the degree to which actors in networks – in particular those who are more centrally placed – actually represent correspondingly important societal interests.

Lessons from Network Analysis

It is not easy to ascertain the lessons to learn from network analysis for the emerging European polity. In the first place, network analysis is by no means the 'handy' theory to deliver ready-made recipes for practical cases. In its main part it is not a theory at all but a kind of generalised description of interactions going on in reality, not intending to go any further than to make out typical patterns and configurations between the 'nodes' of the networks. In the second place, although policy networks do abound in the European arena,[25] they differ from those usually described by the analysis of policy networks in some material points. European networks are, so far, considerably less stable. Their participants display a higher degree of fluctuation as well as of heterogeneity (combining, for instance, lobbyists both from national associations and European groups), and in part lack the problem-solving orientation resulting from a long experience of cooperation. Many of them are themselves less institutionalised and to a lesser degree linked to the institutions of the European decision-making system. In particular, their actions are not in any way embedded into any system of common values and beliefs, nor even based on a jointly shared European identity (see Héritier et al. 1994, p. 9f.).

The lack of stability and the high fluctuation and 'openness' seem to indicate that here, at last, are networks in which indeed any group may participate and whose selectivity can truly be expected to be low. There are several flaws in the matter, though. While access may be principally easy in the sense that hardly any institutional barriers exist, it is not half as easy to ascertain the points of access – both because there are so many of them and because of a general uncertainty about the 'rules of the game'; thus decision-making processes can be said to be 'at once open and opaque' (Mény et al. 1996, p. 14).[26] As a consequence, all these networks seem to have but one 'central actor': the Commission, which is the only actor adequately equipped with information about points of access, rules of the game, etc. The networks therefore can be expected to produce a specific – and rather high – selectivity common to them all. And finally, the linkage between actors in networks and their reference groups or 'home organisations' is considerably more threadbare at European than at the national level, simply because of the greater distance, but also because of the networks' greater internal heterogeneity (with national conflicts cutting across sectoral ones, and vice versa).

25 Witness the large area of 'comitology' described above: those committees are in essence networks, albeit in various stages of formalisation.

26 EU policy making has therefore been likened to the 'garbage can model': 'a system of uncertain agendas, shifting networks and complex coalitions', even of 'organized anarchies', with unpredictable outcomes (Mazey & Richardson 1996, p. 42. See also Mazey & Richardson 1993, Introduction).

The advantage of the Commission's pronounced reliance on policy networks,[27] one might argue, is their basically consensual operation. Their representativity (not to mention the symmetry of interests considered), however, is in doubt. As we have seen, ensuring representativity – and, linked to it, democratic legitimisation – is not only a practical but also a conceptual problem. The dilemma 'democracy versus efficiency' is nowhere as trenchant and tangible as in the case of networks and bargaining systems, for here it seems obvious that an increase in the one directly and inevitably leads to a decline in the other. Networks have evolved, if not to say been invented, expressly in order to improve efficiency: to allow for regulation in societies too complex for state bureaucracies to regulate them any longer. If they are in fact the proper means to achieve the intended aim then ought not efficiency take precedence over democratic requirements – not least since acceptance and legitimacy do rest, in part, on 'good performance'? Unfortunately, such reasoning cannot be applied to the case of the European policy networks (theoretically, at any rate) for so far they lack just the stability on which the argument of superior cooperative efficiency is built.

So one of the few conclusions to be drawn in our context from the theoretical discussion of networks is that it is paramount to install modes of allowing for a modicum of democratic control over their activity. The way in which this can be done has been indicated above: by institutionalising 'connected games' of a certain kind. In many European networks the negotiative game is in fact blurred by being 'nested' into the other one of fixing (or changing) the rules of the game itself, i.e., into the game of constantly revising the treaties. This means that consent to agricultural programmes, for instance, can effectively be traded with that to extensions of majority voting – to the probable detriment to both policy areas, and leaving the baffled public much in the dark about the rationale behind European policies. In contrast, connected games linking network actors periodically – or at times of crucial decisions – to the group they allegedly represent, might help to make decisions more transparent, to reveal the relevant issues and to hold actors accountable – and to prevent the people at the peripheries from being ridden roughshod over.

27 As insiders observe, the Commission in fact encourages networks to be formed wherever possible, not only including various groups but also lower level governments/authorities.

New Normative Democratic Theory

Associative and Reflexive Democracy

In recent years a new variant of 'social democracy' has been debated among political scientists which tries to make out a specific legitimatory role for those groups and associations that have caused so much headache in the discussions of the last two chapters.[28] At the same time, it intends to breathe new life into the ideas of democracy and self-government which appear to have gone stale during the long history of their institutionalised practice. At an early stage of that history, however, some authors already had their doubts about whether a mere 'political' democracy in the shape of elections and parliamentary procedures might not be a poor way to put self-government into effect. Hence the notion of democracy was nearly from the start coupled with demands to extend democratic modes of decision-making to the realms of economy and society.

Under the name of 'associative democracy' (Cohen & Rogers 1992, 1994)[29] this new version of democratic theory argues in a similar vein. It rests essentially on the concept of the 'civil society' which is the new word for the intermediary sphere between the individual and the state – the sphere where the individual combines with others, joins associations, forms notions of a common good transcending his particularistic interests, in short: where he learns to be a 'citizen'. This sphere which is *in nuce* already democratic is singled out for further democratisation by the instalment of new arenas of deliberation, intended to be both instruments of governance (taking over responsibilities of the state) and 'schools of democracy' (Cohen & Rogers 1994, p. 152). Since the existing landscape of associations is deficient in many respects, however, it will have to be remodelled in part. To make it compatible with the democratic ideals of self-government, of competent and reasonable decision-making (enlightened by 'civic consciousness'), and of equality, the formation of new and specific associations will have to be 'encouraged'. No 'egalitarian regime', for instance, will emerge unless all interests found within society are represented; hence 'secondary associations are needed to represent otherwise underrepresented interests.' In other respects,

---

28 Cohen and Rogers (1992, p. 395) explicitly state just this as their main object.
29 For a rather elaborate version of the 'associational welfare state' see also Hirst 1994.

too, 'the right kinds of associations do not naturally arise' and must be 'promoted' by a 'deliberative use of public powers' (ibid., p. 145; see also 1992, p. 422ff.).[30] Although the civil society's associations will then be 'artifactions' for their better part, the authors optimistically expect their members to develop 'new solidarities' *other* than the particularistic solidarities of the pluralist society of old, as well as an 'overlapping consensus' (1994, p. 150ff.) and a public spirit which will enable them to 'govern themselves' in functionally defined arenas of deliberation and decision-making. This is to say that decisions are presumed to result not from bargaining but from deliberative processes, requiring the exchange and discussion of reasons and arguments and allowing for rationally motivated consent.

The version of 'reflexive democracy' (Schmalz-Bruns 1995), while also building on the civil society, is more ready to accept it in its existing shape, concentrating on other devices to instil into its members the public spirit and a proper sense of deliberation. For although 'the citizen' is expressly intended to be returned into his rightful place in the middle of the stage of democratic theory (p. 15), this figure is not identical with the selfish, by particularistic motives driven, individual found in reality: he must be brought to reason, ere he is to occupy his central role. Consequently we again find a comparatively high degree of 'artifaction' and creation. What is to be created – or altered – is, however, rather the constellations between the civil society's groups and associations, instead of these groups and associations themselves.

Yet what is to be altered most of all is the shape, scope, content and procedures of democracy. The democratic process itself is to be made 'reflexive', i.e., to be applied to itself: concerning the 'who' of participation, the 'how' of decision-making and problem-solving, and the 'what' of legitimate political decisions. As in Cohen's concept, this requires a multitude of arenas of deliberation and 'deep-graded processes', set in relation to each other, where the democratic will is to be formed and which are obviously meant to have an educative effect. For the decisions finally reached are not to be considered legitimate unless all those participating have

30 It reads quite simply but one wonders how it will be achieved: 'Where manifest inequalities in political representation exist, associative democracy recommends promoting the organised representation of presently excluded interests. Where group particularism undermines ... democratic deliberation, it recommends encouraging the organised to be more other-regarding in their actions.' – etc. (1992, p. 425)

been ready to apply the principle of 'reflexive revision' to their own preferences and convictions and unless the decisions have been arrived at by force of the better arguments (p. 170ff.). In order to achieve such an ideal state of deliberation, a number of practical devices are proposed, ranging from the reform of parliamentary procedures to the establishment of processes of mediation[31] which can, in part, not easily be reconciled with the professed object of re-installing the citizen in his rightful place at the centre of democracy. Committees of 'disinterested experts', for instance, are to be vested with veto rights to make sure that democratic decisions do not get lost in the maze of particularistic interests and that the right kind of problems are set on the agenda. 'Deliberative opinion polls' are another of the educational measures named. They simulate the opinions a democratic public would embrace if it took the trouble to think rationally and disinterestedly enough about the problems at hand.

Of greater interest here is that the proposal envisages a reduced role of the parliament. In a number of policy areas it will merely decide which policies are to be regulated (and decided upon) centrally or decentrally (p. 177). In the latter case a variety of quasi-political arenas below the parliamentary level and of either a regional or (mainly) a functional nature are called upon to take the relevant decisions. This is where the policy networks come in which in this context appear in the guise of a materialisation of democratic progress. Embedded in distinct 'policy communities', combining all those affected while avoiding a participatory 'over-crowding' of the respective policy arenas (p. 250), they require just a little purgatory effort (regarding the selfishness of their participants) to be acceptable as the ideal associative structures needed for the extension of democracy into the sphere of society. Some 'democratic risks' may accrue from the networks' propensity to exclusiveness and to estrangement from their members. To deal with such weaknesses the figure of a 'mediator' is invented, whose task would be to ensure somehow that all those affected are given their proper chance of participation. In other words, to fit the policy networks into the model of 'reflexive democracy', some constitutional effort is required. Once this effort has been made, the result might well be a kind of multi-dimensional democracy or

---

31 Most of these devices have been first suggested by other authors and are discussed and combined by Schmalz-Bruns to form a compact model for the renewal of democracy.

a democracy of 'variable geometry' (p. 163), in accordance with the variability of functional needs and associative structures.

Other versions of normative democratic theory might be added to these two, resembling them in the major features of (a) conceptualising an ideal world in so far as they suggest that people can be made to behave otherwise than they normally do. In their view they just lack the proper inducements, which gives (b) a highly educational as well as a paternalistic touch to these concepts. Eductional efforts are even more required because (c) these theories are very much concerned with the results and the quality of democratic politics and hence possess a distinct élitist flavour. What they are looking for are new solutions to the (time-honoured) participation–efficiency dilemma of democratic theory, which in these new versions takes the shape (d) of trying to overcome the apparent stagnation of the indirect, representative variants of democracy while avoiding coming too close to any direct form of democracy,[32] since the latter is deemed to be detrimental both to the quality of politics and to the deliberative ideal. The citizen, who is the centre-piece of democratic theory and practice, is to be educated but not to be trusted.

This is not the place to criticise these theories in detail. Suffice it to point out the difficulty of imagining a *democratic* society the associative structure of which was created by 'public powers', which can only mean by the state. Once we discard this notion as being unrealistic as well as somewhat authoritarian, we are left with the conclusion that the pluralist society is to be considered intrinsically democratic and wants little but the (normatively) correct *interpretation* of its members' motives. On the whole, after decades of criticism of the democratic deficiencies of politics leaning heavily on organised interests and of the latter's internal democratic deficits, the normative reassessment of the 'group basis of politics' rather comes as a surprise. One especially wonders why these new concepts, while quite rightly concentrating on the important part groups and networks play in modern governance, forget about the groups' own representativity and democratic structure. As in the concepts of group representation discussed above, the groups are taken for granted and their 'internal affairs' and their relations to reference groups are not called into question. The reason for this omission is, this time, a basic distrust of the individual.

32 Schmalz-Bruns is rather explicit in this; see p. 161.

Lessons from the New Democratic Theories

The material point to be considered here is which lessons are to be learnt from theories of associative or reflexive democracy for the democratisation of the European polity. We may at once lay aside those ideas revolving around the civil society, since by now there is no European civil society worthy of the name. The European federations of national associations are but loosely connected at the top level and lack a European 'body'; they themselves are no associations in the proper sense. We may, however, strike more luckily with regard to the existence of institutions or 'public powers' which might be willing and in a position to create (or just *encourage*) the 'right' associations. Interestingly enough, the Commission has been actually known to induce the formation of some very specific lobbying groups,[33] albeit motivated in this by political ends of its own rather than by a wish to improve democratic self-government. The Commission also encourages the formation of policy networks – as bargaining, not as deliberative arenas, of course. One might thus argue that in a way the Commission does its best to create an associative super-structure in Brussels, which only waits to be complemented by a proper sub-structure and to be 'interpreted' in the right, democratic fashion.

With the notion of the 'variable geometry' of decision-making structures (whether or not enhanced by 'mediators') the concept of reflexive democracy is apparently well adaptable to the complex and multi-dimensional nature of the EU polity. Unfortunately it gives no answers to the question how these factual structures can be made responsive to legitimatory demands. There is little intrinsic democratic value in the associative (and network) structures as such, as long as their representativity is in doubt, and as long as the dealings of the networks at the top lack any visible connection with the wishes and preferences of people at the peripheries. Another question the theory leaves unanswered is the one of boundaries. While it is plausible to suggest policies to be agreed in functionally defined arenas combining those 'affected', we are landed with such thorny problems as how to distinguish the respective arenas (and which criteria to apply), and who and which groups to include; moreover, it remains open who would

33 Grande (1996b, p. 322f.) cites the example of the Commission's having 'created' an industrial lobbying group demanding research programmes in information technology, in order to overcome the Council's resistance to new Community programmes in this area.

decide on the matter of inclusion.[34] In short: all the problems which we have found unsolved in previous chapters crop up again.

The institutional devices suggested by the new normative theories to safeguard the democratic (in part also the egalitarian) quality of group processes tend to build on 'finished' societies with associative structures long established and known to every would-be participant. Concerned with the quality of politics rather than with its participatory features, they also lean heavily on the notion of 'the public' and of 'public opinion' (the tenor of which is to be improved by mediation, simulation, and the like). Unfortunately, neither the one nor the other can be said to exist in European society. One might even argue that there is as yet no such thing as a European society at all. At any rate, European associative structures are very much in flux and at the same time mingled with the various national ones in such a way as to render compositions, constellations, completeness and the like wholly obscure. Nor can we assume the existence of a single public with opinions both known and decisive for actors, and deliberating in a way that could be of any influence upon policy results. Yet if most of the devices proposed may fit the situation of the nation-state rather than that of the European polity, there is one element which looks particularly apt to befit the situation of the latter: the advice to use decision-making powers at central or top level sparingly and to cast the central parliament in the role of a mediating agent which does not decide itself but hands matters to those levels/arenas which seem most concerned or best equipped to deal with the respective issues. Once more, a crucial question remains open: which would be the criteria according to which the parliament would or should thus 'devolve'? There is the other question, of course, why the matters to be decided at lower levels should crop up at the central level, to be handed down again, in the first place. It seems to be a wrong way of subsidiarity, or that of the benevolent centralist.

Conclusion

The various theoretical concepts considered in the preceding chapters do not provide us with a ready-made recipe for the democratisation of a complex non-state polity like the EU; nor did I expect them to do

---

34 The model of Schmalz-Bruns being 'reflexive', the principle of democracy should be applied to these questions. But it remains unclear how this is to be done: by which actors, institutions or arenas.

so. But we can deduce elements from them which may form corner-stones of a model more adequate to deal with the EU's legitimatory problems than the reform proposals debated above.

(1) The first lesson learnt was about decision-making rules. Contractarians are usually called in to justify majority rule as the only one both democratic and 'just' in the sense of producing optimal results. Their arguments in favour of majority rule rest, however, (a) on the notion of a previous 'initial contract' which has been agreed upon unanimously, and (b) on the assumption that contract partners are (or believe themselves to be) fairly equal. Where the latter condition is absent, and where a society is still 'in the making' or in the early stages of formation, no case is to be made for simple majority rule; instead, procedures nearing the unanimity rule are required.

(2) Concerning the allocation of decision-making powers, the main conclusion drawn from fiscal federalism was that in such a society as has just been described, the wisest course to adopt would be to keep it flexible and to allow for the 'recall' of the competences assigned to the top level of governance. It would also seem in general advisable to restrict top-level competences and to leave a high degree of autonomy to lower levels.

(3) Group theories are, unfortunately, of little help for the identification of 'functional groups' or sectoral subunits, although they provide us with the highly interesting concept of 'functional representation'. The 'objective' approach (based on factors such as class, role, industry, or market) does not lead anywhere, and the 'subjective' approach building on the 'all affected' principle leads to trouble. I shall subsequently deal with this matter *in extenso*.

(4) Closely connected to the problem of boundaries between sectoral subunits is that of the representativity and legitimisation of group representatives acting in policy networks. In this respect, the main lesson learnt from network analysis, in combination with game theory, was that there is some need to *systematically* connect the negotiative game within networks with a second game linking the actors firmly to their reference groups.

(5) New normative democratic theory tries to adapt to the complex (network) structure of modern governance but it

provides little help for the reconciliation of this structure with democratic demands, in so far as it relies almost exclusively on deliberative arenas which in the European context are clearly absent. A useful contribution is, however, that parliamentarianism can no longer be the panacea of democratisers, and that existing parliaments are well advised to limit the scope of their activities and leave more room for subunits still to be defined.

Taken all together, these lessons allow but a very cursory answer to the question about the Who, How and What of democracy, raised at the start of our theoretical considerations. Concerning all of the four aspects – the *demos*, the polity, decision-making rules and types of democracy, and the scope of democratic decision-making – the guiding principle of future democratic theory will in fact have to be that of the 'variable geometry'. Its major task will then be to conceive ways to identify and to combine a multiplicity of *demoi*, rules and (sub-) polities.

5

A PROPOSAL FOR
THE DEMOCRATISATION
OF THE EU

The Practical Task

Before submitting my own proposals for the democratisation of the European Union, it seems advisable to recapture briefly what EU policy making looks like at the moment. (1) European decisions are taken by a complex and varying set of actors, comprising institutions with legislative and executive powers (the Commission, the Council, partly the EP as well as the ECJ); institutions of symbolic value and/or with 'advisory' powers (EP, CoR, ESC); and policy networks combining the Commission (always) and various collective actors such as governments, regional authorities, and lobbyists of the most different kinds. (2) Procedures and rules of decision-making in and between these institutions and arrangements vary widely: there is simple majority in the EP; qualified majority in the Council where in such cases the votes are weighted, and in the EP whenever it disagrees with the Council; and unanimity in the Council, in a great number of cases, and as a matter of fact in the policy networks where consensual bargaining instead of outvoting is the rule. (3) Actors within this decision-making set are either 'europeanised' in varying degrees, or national, or subnational, or sectoral (transcending the national distinctions or not). Moreover, they are either governmental or parliamentarian, public or private, collective or even individual actors – and hence obeying wholly different 'logics' of behaviour. (4) They decide matters which do not affect all of them, and their decisions are not applied to all member countries, because of 'opt-outs', 'inner circles', or whatever. (5) These decisions, however, have a 'direct effect' on the peoples of those countries and/or areas which are affected.

This picture of lacking simultaneity of the various dimensions of decision-making, of 'variable geometries' of the most extensive kind, and of wholly uncertain effects, concerning the scope of those affected, presents a very serious challenge for democracy and for democratic theory. If one of the main features of democracy is the congruence of those who participate in decisions and those who are affected by them, then this essence is lost in uncertainty in Europe. Small wonder then that many observers are rather sceptical about the European polity's 'capacity for democracy' (see Kielmansegg 1994, p. 26ff.), and not only because of the absence of a European *demos* and a European identity (see above). More specifically, it seems difficult, if not impossible, to make out definite links between the levels of governance which are democratically legitimised, the levels where actual decisions are taken, and the affected people. Decisions increasingly appear to 'emigrate' from legitimised and would-be autonomous states into supranational relationships, networks, or just '(inter-) dependencies' of varying degrees of visibility and fragility, on the one hand, and to retire into decentralised, quasi-private networks equally opaque and intangible, on the other. The respective *demoi* would then (as Guéhenno 1994 argues, for instance) be either too big still to allow for democracy, or too segmented to be recognisable.

This may well be a general description of the problem of democracy in an age of globalisation. The EU, however, being a halfway house between a supranational state and an international regime, at any rate boasting a comparatively high amount of institutionalisation, offers the chance of proving that the democratisation of non-state governance is yet possible, and thus might pave the way for the 'third transformation' of democracy (Dahl 1989, pp. 2, 320). As Dahl argues, 'a radically new set of political institutions' will be required for this to happen. Otherwise the extension of democracy 'beyond the nation-state' will not take place and we might enter into a new age of 'de facto guardianship' (ibid.) or even of a new 'imperialism' (Guéhenno 1994) instead.

Whatever devices will be invented for the democratisation of the European polity, they will have to meet quite a complex bunch of requirements. (1) In the first place, any institution and/or procedure will have to take account of the fact that the European Union is 'one to be constructed from "old" nations' (Weale 1995, p. 86), with long established political systems, cultures and traditions; hence it should allow for them to continue to exist. Thus the first requirement is the compatibility with the member states' political structures. (2) As we have seen above, the Union is by no means completed up to now, neither in extent (of membership and *demoi*) nor in scope (of policies), nor in the degree of institutionalisation, the formation of policy styles, etc. For a considerable time to come it will remain in a stage of growth and development and, as such, in a state of permanent contractualisation. So the second requirement is to allow for sufficient flexibility since it will need to adapt to continuous change; or, perhaps more precisely, we look for devices suitable to be the means of a kind of 'constant constitutionalisation'.

(3) European policy making occurs both on a territorial basis (decisions taken by governments of states which are, in part, divided into autonomous regional subunits) and on a sectoral basis (policies formulated and implemented by policy networks leaning heavily on 'sectoral experts'). Any of the solutions must be adapted to this multi-dimensionality. Thus the task is to devise ways and means of facilitating accountability not just to European citizens in general, but in particular (and additionally) to citizens on the peripheries, belonging to territorial subunits, whenever they are affected in matters on which the latter's autonomous status rests, as well as to citizens affected in their sectoral interests. (4) Closely connected to the requirement to consider both the territorial and the sectoral dimension of politics is the necessity to provide for a modicum of transparency and accountability of 'network politics'.

(5) A certain amount of flexibility is needed not only because of the Union's incompleteness. There is, moreover, the general democratic requirement of reversibility which includes both the possibility to 'unmake' any laws which have proven detrimental and the right to vote persons out of office. In the European context it is particularly necessary to invent democratic means of the 'recall' of European norms – at least as long as no plausible ways to recall European politicians exist. (6) This list of requirements may be completed by adding that a kind of (quasi-) 'constitutional accomodation to problems of radical diversity' has to be found (Goodin 1996, p. 635). The suitable devices must take into account the extreme heterogeneity of the peoples involved, as well as the low degree of 'Europeanisation' of the citizens.

Constitutions and Contracts

When talking about 'constitutional' elements and 'constitutionalisation' here, I should add that strictly speaking this is only meant in a metaphorical sense. In normal parlance (of continental habits, at least) a constitution is a kind of final contract between a territorially united people, structuring the polity and defining the limits of political authority once and for all. It rests upon a single act of will and intends permanence (which in practice means that constitutional revisions require a considerably higher amount of consent than normal legislative decisions). For the time being, it is impossible to design such a sort of document for the EU. Observers have argued instead that in Europe 'a constitution is progressively being put in place' (PMI 1996, p. 16) but this implies that there is no such thing as a constitution at all: neither is anything definitely fixed, nor has there been a single act of will, let alone by the people. The (quasi-) constitutional elements that might be said to exist as regards structure, institutions and norms have been agreed upon by governments or elaborated by judges – in both cases in a *series* of agreements and decisions which is far from being complete: further series will be required. This process of quasi-constitutionalisation will last for some time to come. Those who advocate the vesting of the union with a constitution at the present time already (as do the EP's Institutional Committee, and its member Fernand Herman in particular) do so in the hope of a serious constitutional debate which would automatically speed up the process of the EU's transformation into a federation. Moreover, they believe that a constitution will provide the European polity even in its present shape with the democratic legitimacy that has so far been lacking. Yet as the first hope is unrealistic, so is the other misplaced. A single act of 'democratic baptism' (Weale 1995, pp. 90 ff.) could not suffice to legitimise a polity *in statu nascendi*, in its yet unfinished state while the process of contractual constitutionalisation is still going on.

This is why I suggest abandoning talk about constitutions in the Union's present state and holding onto the notion of contract. The main reason for this is, of course, that the development of the European polity rests on contracts in actual fact; they just want the inclusion of the people. Furthermore, although constitutions are contracts themselves, ideally, there are some differences between the two which are worth considering here. A constitution is meant to structure a political society already in existence. It builds on a *demos*, on shared culture and traditions, as well as (as we may learn from the more successful instances of constitution building in history) on the presence of a number of crucial and widely accepted socio-political organisations and/or movements; all of which assumes a certain amount of mutual trust. The 'social contract' precedes this stage: it intends to create this political society and triggers off those shared experiences which are a precondition for mutual trust and constitution building. This difference results in another, decisive one, concerning the rules of decision-making and their differentiation. Constitutions normally lay down rules minimising decision-making costs and confine the use of the 'expensive' rule of super-majorities to the (ideally) rare cases of constitutional revision. They distinguish sharply between rules and 'action within rules' (see Brennan & Buchanan 1985, p. 26), reserving the idea of unanimity for the initial decision on the constitution itself (though in history even this decision has usually been taken by majorities). In contrast, the notion of contract implies – in theory as well as in everyday practice – the requirement of the consent of *all* parties to it. Contracts may also lay down decision-making rules other than unanimity for certain matters enumerated in it, but according to their own logic they cannot do so for subsequent contracts. In a succession of contracts, the consent of *all* will be required, each time anew.

The Elements of the Proposal

Having set out the task and listed the requirements any model for the democratisation of the EU will have to meet, I shall in the remainder of this chapter outline just such a proposal. This is mainly a system of direct-democratic veto rights, the basic features of which will be explained in the next section. The following section will enlarge upon the subject of the regional veto, to be restricted to the matter of assignment of competences. The sectoral veto and the thorny problem how to distinguish respective units (a problem left unsolved in the preceding theoretical survey) will be dealt with next.

Having found at least a tentative solution to the problem I can then proceed, in the following section, to turn to the more practical questions of how the respective referenda should be organised: which types of referenda are suggested; who could set them in motion; which majorities ought to be met; to which types of decisions they are to be applied to; which effect they might have on European policies. Some more or less fictitious examples will finally illustrate how the proposed system of veto rights could work.

A System of Veto Rights

A *'Contract in Being'*

The notion of contract is particularly apt to depict the character of European law making, not only because the latter is based on a series of contracts in actual fact, but also because it rests on various types of contracts which are interconnected in complex ways. There is (1) the 'initial contract' constituting the European Community, now Union, agreed upon 'vicariously' by member-state governments; this initial contract has been and is being revised and amended in a series of summits and Intergovernmental Conferences, lately with increasing velocity. In many cases the governments have not thought it necessary to ask their people's assent, either initially or at one or other crucial stages of quasi-constitutional development, deeming their own vicarious actions sufficiently legitimised by (2) the constitutional contracts of member states. Rights and procedures agreed in them (and subsequently guaranteed by them) are, however, systematically exposed to infringement by the contracts of type 1. One should add that associations taking part in EU decision-making in their own right found their actions on a similar kind of 'initial contract' (in the shape of their statutes). Yet type 2 contracts are liable to be violated not only by those of type 1. Furthermore, what may be named (3) the 'every-day contracts' (i.e., the EC's secondary law), resulting from the negotiations of member-state governments in the Council (in part also from the negotiations in multi-level networks if subsequently rubber-stamped by the institutions proper), are frequently, in content and effect, of the same quality as type 1 contracts, albeit perhaps to a lesser degree and, at any rate, less visibly. They infringe upon type 2 contracts mainly (though not exclusively) by gradually expanding the range of European policies.

As has been mentioned above, the distinguishing feature of contracts is that the consent of all partners is needed for them to come into existence: they require unanimity. But European practice so far has clearly deviated from this principle considerably. The principle of unanimity has been preserved in type 1 contracts only, and even there it is in danger of becoming weakened. In type 3 contracts its application is restricted to a decreasing number of cases. On the other hand, the effects of both on type 2 contracts are rarely recognised as revisions of the latter, requiring higher majorities than usual, let alone unanimity. And of course, even where unanimity is in fact prescribed, formally (in the IGCs and, in part, in the Council) or informally (in networks), it is only that of corporate actors: of executives and authorities of various kinds.

If EU decision-making is (as I am arguing here) to be interpreted as an 'initial contract in being', then the principle of unanimity embodied in this notion has to be properly respected. At the same time, this principle then cannot be applied exclusively to representatives. Furthermore (and as we may learn from contractarians), the principle is the more strictly to be adhered to in cases of great heterogeneity.[1] The European societies are heterogeneous to the extent that no genuine 'European majority' can be said to exist; instead there is a bundle of minorities (mirrored, in part, by the segmented nature of the EP as well as of the European quasi-party system). Although the EP appears to be clearly dominated by a kind of permanent (inter-party) 'great coalition' of those (inter-state party) coalitions named the European People's Party (EPP) and the European Socialist Party (ESP), this coalition is inherently negative in character in the first place, because it blocks motions originating in the EP itself[2] (which is of rather a 'positive' effect for the Commission, however, enabling it to push forth with its policies unhampered by parliamentary control). In the second, it is not based on a respective segment of the European peoples united by the same wish to further European integration or by any other shared values or interests. So far this 'great coalition' is as artificial as it is contingent, as in fact any other coalition of the various minorities, emerging in one case or the other, would be. They would mostly have to be characterised not by what unites them but by what they lack: any bond which might turn a mere passing constellation into a closer alliance. The endowment of such ephemeral or artificial majorities with the power to decide over the future of the whole conglomerate (decision-making rules, allocation of competences, and all), in a stage when it is still in the process of growing into some sort of polity, seems to be a high-risk strategy and bodes ill for future acceptance and legitimacy.[3]

1   See also Lane's (1996) 'theorems' about which structures of society do not allow for 'minimalist democratic institutions' characterised by simple majority voting (p. 245ff.).
2   Frequently, recommendations by EP committees, i.e., by the EP's own 'experts', are thus blocked in the plenum. The rejection of a motion of non-confidence against the Commission in the 'BSE affair' is a case in point, as the EP's final stance concerning 'Novel food' (see below).
3   See also Dehousse (1995, p. 131): 'the democratisation of the European political system can only be achieved through the setting up of a pluralist, non-majoritarian model...'.

The Double Requirement Of Unanimity And Direct Democracy

I have just been sketching the situation of majorities of representatives deciding in heterogeneous societies, with the factor of a 'polity in the making' aggravating matters. The resulting problem of lacking acceptance, or so it seems, can be expected to be solved by the *consensual* decision-making of representatives, as used to be the rule in the Council. The main criticism of decision procedures requiring unanimity is that they are highly inefficient and unduly expensive since they result in complicated bargaining processes including package-deals, log-rolling, side-payments, or 'pork-barrel' solutions: if A, B and C are to give their consent to a particular decision which benefits them unevenly, those benefiting less understandably wish to be compensated somehow – either in cash (one of the reasons why subsidising has become so ubiquitous) or by concessions in some other decision. In the present context, however, the stumbling block is less that such decision-making is in fact quite costly, but rather that this particular mode of arriving at priorities and of shaping policies (even polities, as in the case of the EU!) is not very likely to meet with high acceptance: it does not solve the problem(s) it has been intended to solve.

Four reasons, at least, may be given for this. (1) The complex compromises and package-deals, arrived at in delicate and necessarily non-public negotiations, cannot easily be explained to people on the peripheries whose interests seem to have been thwarted. (2) Those people cannot even be sure that their interests will be dealt with by another part of the 'package'; instead they may well suspect that their representatives – as government members – will pursue both institutional and personal interests of their own.[4] (3) Democratic procedures 'at home', short of motions of no-confidence, will be of little help because negotiators can convincingly argue that no better result could have been achieved, and that the present government had better not be disavowed in this – that is: there is hardly any way of effective *ex-post* control in such cases. (4) Nor will 'legitimisation by performance', i.e., by effective problem-solving, provide a sort of substitute, for with this mode of bargaining the adequacy of solutions for actual problems is very much a matter of contingency, too.

---

4 A good illustration for this is the way the German *Bundesrat* operates: composed of members of *Länder* governments, it maximises the latters' influence in federal politics, quite careless (in part at least) of the interests of *Länder* citizens.

So we end up with the conclusion that at the EU's present stage of 'iterated initial contracts' crucial decisions ought to be taken (1) unanimously and (2) directly, i.e., by directly involving the various European peoples. This double requirement is less utopian than it sounds on first hearing. In the first place, it should always be borne in mind that the unanimity required is that of those *affected*, and in the second, that for unanimity to be achieved it is not necessary that everybody's assent to every single decision has to be obtained. Unanimity can be reached *ex negativo* instead by vesting the groups, units or minorities making up a heterogeneous society with the right to dissent. One of the lessons to be learnt from federalism as well as from corporatism and consociationalism is that there are generally two ways of dealing with 'radical social diversity': 'One strategy is to assign each distinctive group a separate sphere within which it will enjoy autonomous decision-making power. The other is for all decisions to be made collectively but to give all the distinctive groups veto power over those collective decisions' (Goodin 1996, p. 639). The normal course of events would be to combine these two, bearing in mind that there is a trade-off between them; hence the importance of group vetoes will increase the less autonomy is left to those groups. Yet granting veto rights only to group representatives leads to élite cartels, with all the negative consequences alluded to above. Up to a certain degree both élite cartels and bargaining systems are unavoidable in heavily segmented societies. It is even more decisive then to provide for 'democratic outlets' and to firmly install a 'second game', binding the élites back to those who they are supposed to represent. Since the dealings of élite cartels are opaque and the representative quality of the élites' dealings systematically in doubt, no version of 'implicit consent' will do in this respect. Nothing will suffice but the opportunity for people to contradict those at the top directly – that is: the direct-democratic veto right.

The veto powers in existence until now are, apart from being assigned rather exclusively to governments (with some very rare exceptions, like the national referenda on the Maastricht Treaty), by statute strictly limited to the member states. In principle, there seems to be little sense in enhancing the dominating role of nation-states in EU politics any further by coupling the governmental veto in the Council or at summits with nation-wide referenda. On the other hand, there is a good case for opening up this possibility by statute, for governments of the day have been known to pursue other lines than their public would wish them to do. The promotion of national referenda is not my primary object here; whether or not, and when they ought to be held is a question which one should think may safely be left to the care of nation-states themselves, more precisely: to the actors of the national political systems. The chances of nation-wide majorities to hold their governments responsible (albeit not on single issues) and to vote them out of office are in most countries by no means negligible. To such optimism one may well add the pessimistic assessment, easily to be corroborated by empirical data, that national referenda are very likely to be exploited for purposes of national party politics. If national referenda are to be included in the system of veto rights at all (for the sake of its completion) they will have to be designed with special care.

The case is different with national subunits and with groups 'cutting across nations and nation-states, with constituencies defined according to the nature and scope of controversial transnational issues' (Held 1991, p. 283). It might not bother nation-wide majorities at all if the interests of these subunits and groups are thwarted; or these interests may seem to run counter to the 'national interest' as defined by these (party-) political majorities; in part, the latter may not even be aware of the problem. At the same time, the participation especially of transnational groups in European decision-making might be one of the rare occasions to bring the ranges of participating, bearing costs and benefiting more into line with each other, i.e., to come closer to the 'congruence' increasingly lost in the national context.

Hence the suggestion is to grant the direct-democratic veto primarily to territorial units below national level and to sectoral units cross-cutting it. The first (or territorial) veto is to be considered mainly as a solution to one of the EU's major compatibility problems. Those territorial subunits which had managed to have their core values protected and their right of self-government constitutionally entrenched within nation-states have suffered from European integration in a twofold way: the spheres of autonomy guaranteed at the national level have not been safe from infringement by the higher level, nor has their right to democratic self-government been respected, in that the powers of their parliaments have been drastically reduced. They ought to be given a right to contradict any such development, in case their people wish to see their autonomy reasserted. The second (or sectoral) veto is supposed to be the answer to various of the EU's legitimatory problems. It may defuse the incompatibility problem since it helps 'old' participatory rights to survive and can generally be expected to enhance democratic participation. It can also be an answer to the question of how to democratise bargaining systems, and to that of how to deal with a growing but yet incomplete 'Europeanness'. Moreover, it may contribute (as has just been mentioned) to the solution of the pervasive problem of contemporary democracies, whether at European or at national level: the increasing incongruence.

Together both vetoes represent a mode of democratisation paying due respect to the multi-dimensionality of EU policy making and to the 'variable geometry' of integration. They allow for the high degree of flexibility needed in a polity not yet complete and too complex to make normal constitutionalisation possible, but will all the same provide a means to hold actors at European level accountable to the people on the peripheries. Furthermore, the proposed device can easily be added to the EU's existing institutional set-up without causing any grave disturbances to those acting in it. They will not be exposed to any greater inconvenience than that of being taken to task over their decisions and of being held accountable with respect to them in a more direct and visible way than they used to be.

Regional Subunits: The Assignment Of Powers

The 'Federalist Problem'

The main interest of territorial subunits will be to preserve their autonomous legislative powers; these, in their turn, are the shield to protect the regional groups' values and interests, which are supposed to be diverse enough to be in need of such protection. The division of powers between territories, or regions, and the central state is one of the key features of federalism. Hence any political scientist would tell us that the adequate political structure for territorially segmented societies – and in particular of nations formed from segments with an own political tradition – is a federation; and most of them would stop there. But federalism is not yet the answer to the problems of such societies; rather it is a starting point for asking the right questions. As we have already seen, there are various models of federalism, differing especially in the way powers are divided; indeed in some models they are not divided at all.

The conclusions drawn from the theoretical considerations concerning federalism (above) have also been far from clear-cut. The major lesson taught by the theory of fiscal federalism is that competences ought to be assigned to the various levels of jurisdiction according to the principle of homogeneity of preferences, which is only another version of the principle to bind the right of decision to the consent of those who are affected by the decisions. This rule, however, is not applicable to all kinds of policies, not to mention the practical problem of finding out for any policy at any given time whether sufficiently widespread agreement exists with regard to it, and at which level(s) of government. Hence the obvious difficulty, in theory as well as in practice, of inventing modes of distributing competences, or of drawing up separate catalogues of competences, that are plausible, convincing, durable and practicable. Another reason for the same problem is the interdependence of policy areas and, consequently, of the fulfilment of public tasks. According to many (if not most) of the fiscal federalists any policy that (a) causes spill-overs and (b) has (re-)distributive effects, or (c) would in the 'nature of things' require cooperation, has to be assigned to the central (federal) state; in reality, this does not leave the regions much to do. One might conclude then that federalist theory is generally not of much help to the interests of territorial subunits.

Another lesson, however, was that in sharply segmented societies the assignment of powers to the top level ought to be handled with the utmost care (although it has to be added that the theory of fiscal federalism is by no means unequivocal on this point). To justify such a transfer of powers, neither the argument of the central state's superior 'system capacity' should suffice, nor the hazy notion that action taken by the Union might 'better attain the purposes intended' (as Art. 3 b TEC suggests). Instead, additional proof of actual spill-overs should be required at least. As the ECG proposes (1993, I, V p.4), 'individual or group action by Member States must be shown to have caused substantial material damage to at least one other Member State'. Of course, there are policies where central responsibility seems to go without saying like, for instance, trade policies and environmental protection. But even there problems will inevitably arise when – as is typically the case in the latter policy area – preferences as to the What, How and How Much vary widely between subunits; or, in other words, when two of the principles of fiscal federalism come into conflict. Giving precedence to the unanimity rule, such conflicts can be solved in the way that top-level decisions on the respective issues are to be strictly limited to the fixing of minimum levels (*'Mindestniveaugarantie'*), leaving it to the lower levels to realise higher standards if they wish. Following the federalist principle of subsidiarity, top level jurisdiction should generally be confined to frameworks (guidelines), anyway.

Maxims such as these are nonetheless poor guides when it comes to the practical task of allocating competences not only between two levels (federal state and component units, or Community and member states), but between three of them (adding that of member states' subunits). Yet the resulting problem is not just the greater complexity. The theory of fiscal federalism is mainly concerned with questions of efficiency, aiming at the Pareto-optimal procurement of public goods, rather than with questions of legitimate decision-making, democratic participation, and the protection of regional autonomy and 'collective identity'. Somehow, requirements of the latter kind will have to qualify the findings of fiscal federalism. As a consequence, one may well end up with the general conclusion that many of those policy areas which on the face of them cry for harmonisation may, at a second glance, safely be left to the care of decentral agencies, after all (see Blöchliger & Frey 1992, p. 540f.).[5]

Apparently, the 'federalist problem' is primarily not one of finding the *one* plausible principle of unambiguous distribution of powers between two or more levels of government, but one of finding the proper balance between the need for effective governance, at any of those levels and in the interest of all the parts of the respective society, on the one hand, and the wish to retain regional autonomy and self-government, on the other. The balance will vary with the intensity of conflict between regions or between centre and periphery, according to the degree to which the sense of regional distinctness is rooted in the people's minds, with the virulence of their wish for separateness, etc. The first question to ask with respect to federalism, therefore, is not how to achieve Pareto-efficiency but about the degrees and types of distinctness. And with regard to them it is less the objective heterogeneity that matters than their subjective correlates: the *awareness* of distinction,

---

5   As Scharpf has argued (1994a, p. 227ff.), the best way to achieve (for instance) the technical co-ordination and standardisation called for in a Single Market, is by no means necessarily to maximise uniformity by EU norms, but could consist of the mere provision of incentives for the voluntary agreement of 'mutual adaptation in the market' (p. 231).

the *consciousness* of a tradition of independence, the *wish* for separate self-government. The last-mentioned may be very pronounced in regions of comparatively little socio-cultural diversity, while people in regions differing widely, objectively, may display an equally pronounced propensity for harmonisation and for 'uniform conditions of life'.

Where preferences such as the wish for a uniformity of welfare dominate, there will be little sense in dividing powers, and federalism will, in fact, mean little more than a mode of decentralisation and an allocational device; and to reach efficiency may be considered a mere technical matter. Where the sense of distinctiveness prevails, however, – which it might well do in cases of a long tradition of political independence – considerations of efficiency will have to stand back. Instead, the primary concern will have to be how to maintain regional self-government as intact as possible, in the teeth of increasing interdependence, and even on 'third levels'. Endeavours to achieve this object will have to bear in mind two things: (1) Any constitutionally fixed catalogue of competences, involving several levels, will as likely as not (and especially in an economic area as closely interwoven as the European one) raise nearly as many practical problems as the general interconnection of powers would do – with the one possible caveat that in the first case the problem will mainly be the lacking efficiency, while in the second this same kind of problem will be augmented by the violation of the territorial (sub-)units' rights; hence specific 'frustration costs' will have to be added to the costs accruing from (allocative) inefficiency. (2) Howsoever the matter of the assignment of competences will be dealt with: the last word should rest with those units whose right of self-government is at stake, instead of top-level officials and 'technocrats' aiming at streamlined policy making.

The Requirement Of Flexibility

With these presuppositions in mind, there seems only one solution left for a complex (con-) federalist polity like the EU. Whether the present, somewhat expansive assignment of powers to the Union level is maintained for the time being; or whether powers are allocated anew in a more logical and especially in a more restrictive manner; or whether even a 'bipolar' catalogue of competences is compiled (as proposed by Scharpf 1994a and by the ESK; see above): the material point is to keep any such distribution *flexible*, which means opening it for contradiction and recall. The ECG (to whom I have already alluded frequently) have suggested 'repatriating' powers when member states 'find that collective action is not successful or that individual action by Member States may be just as effective'; for 'views on what functions are best carried out by Member States themselves, or by Member States acting collectively as a Union, or in a broader international framework will change over time.' They criticise the 'one-way dynamic' embodied in the treaty and in the notion of the 'acquis communautaire' and recommend instead that Union powers should be reviewed periodically and be 'repatriated' eventually if deemed necessary, in procedures 'less cumbersome' than those normally applied to revisions of the treaty.[6] They are, however, reticent about what the 'less cumbersome' ways should be like.

The recall of powers I suggest here differs from the ECG proposal mainly in two ways. In the first place, it is intended to complement it, applying the principle of 'repatriation' of powers also to those regional subunits which used to enjoy autonomous status and the legislative powers of which tend to get lost (or have been lost already) in the European maze. Secondly, I consider it unwise to leave the matter of recall or repatriation to governments who in that respect cannot be trusted, as the German example may illustrate (see above). The loss of competences is a trifle for governments, as long as their own influence (institutional as well as personal) upon the process of decision-making of higher levels is guaranteed: they just trade one against another kind of influence. The loss is, however, a grievous one for parliaments and, as regards their shared values and interests, perhaps even more so for the people on the peripheries. Hence the suggestion of vesting the people of regional units of autonomous status with the right of revocation, concerning any legislative power of theirs that has meanwhile been assigned to the European level, whether overtly (by treaty) or clandestinely (by ECJ rulings, implied powers, or whatever). In order to prevent misunderstanding: this right should indeed be strictly confined to cases of the loss or infringement of decision-making powers which before had been unequivocally allocated at the regional level.

In the case of the regional units the direct-democratic veto should be generally restricted to this question of legislative powers. It would, of course, be more than a mere veto, in so far as it is not

6   ECG 1993, 'Draft Statement of Constitutional Principles' 9, p. 10.

solely directed against any move to grant new powers to the Union, but includes the recall. The extension appears necessary because of this tendency just mentioned, to expand Community powers without openly declaring the respective step to be one of altering the distribution of powers, a step which in any 'normal' federation would require some formal revisionary procedure. In the absence (up to now) of any properly passed list of community powers, disputes about them will inevitably occur on an *ad hoc* basis; hence both the recall and the veto against additional powers will frequently take the shape of a veto against or revocation of a particular policy, already enacted or due to be so, which clearly touches upon the regional units' spheres of self-government.

Incidentally, despite their apparent logic the specific regional veto and recall must not be equated with a 'brake' or mere blocking power as regards 'active governance', but can have quite the opposite effect. The European policies subjected to the veto are, more often than not, those of ending (national) regulation and political intervention, i.e., decisions forcing authorities to leave matters to self-regulation by the markets. In blocking them, the veto would in fact enable authorities at lower levels to pursue more active policies.[7] This indicates that European politics, and its multi-level character in particular, are far too complex to allow for an easy classification of any single political device as having 'negative' (blocking) or 'positive' (active and innovative) effects.

It should nevertheless be noted that the proposed veto makes for a somewhat skewed federalism. Not any region anywhere in Europe would benefit, since not all of them would be entitled to undertake moves to restrict or revoke Community powers, but only regions with formal autonomy; for only those that possess competences of their own can suffer violation of them and, hence, be endowed with the right to defend them. Of course the device would merely accentuate an existing asymmetry, instead of creating it. It is an indisputable fact that regions in Europe differ widely in status, autonomy and self-administration. Any device dealing with the role and rights of regions must take account of these differences. Therefore, after a closer look at least, it should be regarded as an advantage that the proposed system of veto rights, in not asking for new and additional institutions (like a 'Senate of Regions', for instance) does not itself require equality of status and

---

7   Direct-democratic vetoes at times do actually work this way. On 1 December 1996, for instance, the Swiss people rejected a Bill that intended to water down working-time regulations.

simultaneity of development. Leaving for the time existing diversity as it is it allows at the same time for (nearly) any kind of flexibility, including the one that any region acquiring autonomous status in future would, quasi-automatically, then also be endowed with those veto rights. In mid-term, this may even prove to be an incentive for the further regionalisation of member states – in fact, for the gradual emergence of a 'Europe of the Regions'.

Sectoral Subunits: How To Distinguish Them

Democratising Networks

Neither governance nor administration are by necessity territorially based. Hence the concepts of (neo-) corporatism, of 'functional democracy' (Cole), or of 'non-territorial federalism' (Elkins 1995, p. 147ff.) are based upon sectoral (political) units which are arguably even less symmetric, homogeneous, or of equal status. Yet what I propose here is to vest the members of such units with political rights in European policy making similar to those of territorial units. At the present stage the sectoral dimension of politics is embodied in the manifold policy networks (in those of them, that is, which are not exclusively composed of government members of the various levels), advising the Commission in the formulation of sectoral policies and helping to implement them. They do partake, more or less extensively, in European decision-making without themselves openly inviting participation: participation in sectoral networks is limited to relatively few 'experts', managers, and lobbyists who are all privileged by their position in associations, their contacts, knowledge about points of access, and other informal if not dark means and channels. The comparatively great influence of the lobbyists and administrators (of the most various kinds) who form the networks may in part be explained by the gradual 'maturing' of European policy making under conditions of a lacking European public and a lacking 'interested electorate'. This has led to processes of routinisation of 'interest politics' in the narrowest sense and to apparent depoliticisation, which in their turn brought forth 'in-group feelings' and a sort of special 'socialisation' of the (originally national, of course) experts and lobbyists (see Kerremans 1996, p. 231ff.), alienating them from their reference groups 'at home'. In effect, these group representatives by now represent hardly anyone else but themselves. It is high time, one should think, to re-politicise their dealings by 'bringing the people back in' (see Hedetoft 1994, p. 143), and to invent means to hold networks and the actors within them accountable.

A second problem attached to the great influence of issue networks in the European arena is their lopsidedness. In principle they may be an appropriate means to reflect the objective links and interdependencies existing between various segments of society, organisations and administrations, concerning a specific issue, and to bring together all those with a stake in the matter and join them in a common effort, resulting in a policy or regulation benefiting all sides. In practice, however, these networks are bilateral more often than multilateral; more precisely: while they typically combine various (organised) producer interests, they tend to neglect the interests of those affected by their decisions, i.e., (mostly) the consumer side. In part this asymmetry is due to the lack of organisation on the side of 'those affected' who are, in all likelihood, rather an amorphous or motley quasi-group, compared with the producers, united by a specific common if not narrow interest. But even the more influential and well organised non-governmental organisations (like Greenpeace, Friends of the Earth and the like) which have sprung up in the meantime, are not admitted to such issue networks; instead they act as a kind of self-styled opposition, attacking and criticising from the outside.

Issue networks thus obviously have some considerable drawbacks, as regards the representativity, transparency and inclusiveness of their dealings. On the other hand, they have the definite advantage of being cross-national and in fact highly 'europeanised' actors. Hence the task is to find remedies for the drawbacks while maintaining the advantage: to make them accountable and correct asymmetries without taking recourse to the nation-state level. The network actors' negotiative game has to be complemented by a 'connected game' that (a) makes them visible in the first place, (b) links them firmly to depictable sectors of society (and to the reference groups they profess to represent), (c) gives those who had been bypassed up to that point the chance to have their views included, and (d) allows the whole sectoral interrelationship to find some sort of legitimacy of its own, independent of the mechanisms legitimising group politics in nation-states (which is mainly the national electoral linkage). The answer to this puzzle is a sectoral veto fashioned after the model of the 'optional referendum'. It has to meet two basic requirements: the respective 'sectoral *demos*' would have to be cross-national, and it would have to include 'all those affected' or, in market-like constellations, both sides of the market.

After what has been said above, the prerequisite of inclusiveness should not be in need of further explaining; it follows from the principles of justice, fairness and 'equality of opportunities'. But the cross-national character required of the 'sectoral *demos*' may come as a surprise to readers who are used to think in the terms of traditional, i.e., national democracy. They are to be reminded that a mere doubling of the national (territorially-based) influence on European policies is what is intended least by the invention of the sectoral veto. In fact, as has already been mentioned, European issue networks tend to operate as 'europeanised' actors and may be assumed to form the nucleus of the civic infrastructure so far lacking in Europe. If the alleged reference groups of network actors (as well as those suffering from their actions) could be brought to realise that they have (sectoral) interests in common which cross-cut national boundaries, the emergence of a European 'civil society' might be sped up. Apart from this maybe idealistic hope the prerequisite follows from the principle of congruence: if decisions increasingly affect parts of the European society which are not territorially defined, then such non-territorial, *non-national demoi* ought to have the right to participate.

The 'Boundary Problem'

As soon as one has stated the two maxims governing the formation of a sectoral unit, the 'demarcation disputes' begin (Goodin 1996, p. 640). For 'all those affected' can mean anything; in particular, it can be interpreted in a way to include nearly everybody, nearly always. 'All those affected' taken literally is not of much use as a distinguishing mark of sectors; in a manner of speaking, a maxim like this would transform any good into a 'collective good', for the consumption of nearly every good produces some external effect or other, if one only looks closely enough.

As we have seen in the last chapter it is not only exceedingly difficult to distinguish sectoral entities but it is virtually impossible to do so by using *objective* criteria. Yet even if there were plausible ways to define sectoral boundaries, to rely on these would not suffice when it comes to the matter of democratisation; for to become included in a self-governing *demos*, the essential point is whether or not an individual 'identifies'. If we are looking for respective 'collective identities', the relevant criteria are subjective ones. The 'all-affected' principle will then have to be re-defined as 'all those who *feel* affected', which might be further accentuated as those who share the same risks and are intensely *aware* of it.

It is debatable whether or not the combination of objectively shared risks and subjective awareness will provide a bond sufficient for the constitution of a 'collective identity'. Most social philosophers would tend to argue that, in addition, 'shared values' were required. The notion of common values, however, presupposes a modicum of shared traditions and, hence, interrelationships or even entities of longer duration and of more stable character than can be assumed to exist in any transnational sectoral context. Moreover, one of the objects of bringing in the 'sectoral *demoi*' at all was to meet the legitimatory requirements (1) of the as yet unfixed, unstable, fleeting interrelations in an emerging polity and (2) of the 'by nature' fluid, in part even ephemeral character of issue-related political constellations. Any device to democratise sectoral or issue bargaining systems will have to take account of the fact that their composition will vary, and that whatever their (two- or multi-sided) reference groups are considered will be subject to frequent change. The requirement of subjective identification had therefore better not be exaggerated, lest the gains in flexibility which the notion of sectoral entities promises be lost. This is why Elkins' suggestion (1995, p. 167ff.) that we identify non-territorial 'unbundled communities' by their members' awareness of mutual dependence and resulting 'mutual responsibility', albeit plausible (particularly since this allows for the integration of competing and even conflicting interests), befits corporatist systems rather than a conglomerate of policy networks.

So we end up with an apparent conundrum: territorial units are marked by a definite 'sense of belonging' although their members' interests are typically very diverse; in contrast, sectoral units may have shared interests and shared risks (denoting the 'other side') as a starting point but mostly lack this 'sense of belonging' and hence the quality of being politically recognisable. In order to establish who the varying *demoi* are in the sectoral dimension of politics, Whelan (1983, p. 19) argues that 'before a democratic decision could be made on a particular issue ... a prior decision would have to be made, in each case, as to who is affected and therefore entitled to vote on the substantive issue – a decision, that is, on the proper bounds of the relevant constituency.' Whelan himself judges this to be an impossible task, thus (implicitly) adding up to the numerous authors deeming issue networks or bargaining systems systematically not fit to be rendered democratic. However, what in the eyes of Whelan is an insoluble problem may simply boil down to an empirical matter.

Empirical Pre-Tests?

There are different means of finding out empirically who considers himself to belong to a 'sectoral constituency', at any given time, each more or less laborious and costly, and each possessing some drawbacks. (1) The simplest but least adequate mode (as I have already argued above) would be to count the members of all the associations which appear to constitute a functional sector of the united European societies and the representatives of which participate in the respective networks. Apart from being simple, it would have the further advantage of providing comparatively stable *demoi*, for the same organised interests would be concerned with – and feel affected by – quite a number of different issues. However, not all those affected are organised, particularly (and typically) not those who 'share the risks' or have to pay the costs (literally as well as figuratively). Hence this device would prolong and even intensify the major weakness of issue networks, instead of curing it: their basic asymmetry. Nor is it possible, by this means, to consider *ad hoc* groups, not organised yet quasi-united by feeling rather strongly about some particular issue.

(2) A second and more flexible way to identify relevant sectoral groups is the 'voucher' system proposed by Schmitter (*inter alia*) and briefly introduced in the preceding chapter. It could operate more flexibly in so far as citizens would be called upon periodically to decide on their allegiances to particular associations; thus sizes of reference groups, boundaries between them as well as between sectors over a period of time might be shown to vary considerably. The major drawback is, again, the organisational bias. Although by this means the wider halo of 'identifiers', around the core of those who actually join the associations of their choice, could be included in the notion of sectoral unit, issue-related *ad hoc* groups and loose 'social movements' are still excluded.

In order to allow for the inclusion of such issue-related 'identifiers' and thus to complete the reference basis of issue networks, there seems nothing left but 'to ask people'. This could be done (3) by way of a kind of pre-test, analogous to the primaries in which American citizens may declare their party allegiance. This declaration then entitles them to participate in the (inner-party!) process of selection of candidates for the election. Whenever a sectoral veto had been initiated, people might likewise be called upon to register, declaring their interest in the matter at hand. By intent, such a 'primary' would differ from a public petition demanding a referendum to be held in two decisive aspects. In the case of the petition, signatures are collected until a required quorum is reached;[8] typically, only those will register who represent one side of the dispute, i.e., who either oppose or demand a particular act or regulation. In contrast, in the case of the primary both sides would be called upon to register; and in an ideal world they would do so either as completely as possible, or in similar proportions, to give an inkling of the size of the potential sectoral unit. The first version could be enforced by the simple device that only those who have registered before are allowed to vote afterwards. But such a mere doubling of the effort would appear somewhat pointless, for the knowledge gained would amount to no more than that those who vote will vote. In the second version, activists of both sides would be expected to register, and in doing so would have to declare the side on which they stand. It would then be the task of electoral experts (some sort of 'electoral commission') to guess from the number and type of registered activists on the probable size of the whole group. With this rough knowledge of the size of the unit the same commission could then decide upon the majority needed for this particular veto to become effective. As likely as not, this procedure would induce all the associations with a stake in the matter to tell their members to behave strategically, that is, not to register all of them so that it would be the easier to win a (accordingly smaller) majority in the referendum proper. Of course such strategies could be counterbalanced (a) by the probability of the strategies of various associations neutralising each other and (b) by the danger that the whole number of registered persons might remain below a threshold of negligibility still to be defined (see below). Whatever the course adopted, the whole business would seem rather cumbersome and the information gained about the likely size of the potential groups either trivial or uncertain. One should therefore judge the considerable effort and costs as misplaced.

The Optional Referendum

Apparently, we look in vain for a device both theoretically convincing and practicable. In this case there is but one option left: to trust that those who 'identify' and/or feel strongly about the matter at hand will, in fact, be those who go to the ballot box. So far, our considerations have yielded the result that a sectoral unit,

8 Cf. the Swiss practice: here the signatures of 50,000 citizens are needed before a parliamentary act is to be subjected to the popular vote.

however, fluid it may be, consists (1) of a core of activists, i.e., citizens organised in respective associations, albeit of (at least) two sides, most generally to be marked as those who benefit and those who bear the costs; and (2) of a wider circle (of varying extents) of those who 'share the interests' and 'share the risks'; the one stipulation for the latter to be included in the sectoral *demos* was (3) that they are – more or less intensely – aware of these shared interests and risks. Now we may add: (4) they must be so intensely aware of them as to be prepared to act accordingly. For those especially who do not belong to the side of producers (in the widest sense), 'being prepared to act' can mean a host of things, of course – to demonstrate, to boycott certain products or retailers, to block transports, to form human chains, to send off postcards, and the like. A not very demanding but nevertheless decisive kind of activity is that of participating in a referendum.

The practical experience with referenda in the few countries where they are frequent[9] (and, what is also important, not initiated by the authorities) tells us that it is rarely an overall majority that decides – and even participates – but normally an 'interested minority'. Direct democracy, we are informed, 'does not rely on the will of the whole people but on the expressed preferences of a minority' (Linder 1994, p. 92). And while some analysts of the Swiss political system are convinced that the instruments of direct democracy have resulted in an exceedingly high influence of interest associations (Neidhart 1970), empirical data show that the organised groups cannot be at all sure of their influence in any particular referendum, and that these instruments at the same time provide *ad hoc* groups with opportunities they could not dream of in any other system (Möckli 1994, p. 234ff., 241ff.).

Although there is no unambiguous empirical evidence (apparently because of a lacking interest on the part of researchers until now)[10] that referenda unite, as a rule, both sides of a political controversy[11], I think we may safely assume that whenever turnout

9 See Möckli 1994; Linder 1994, p. 91ff.; Butler & Ranney 1994, p. 134ff., 242ff.

10 Empirical research concentrates primarily on the features of the average regular voter and abstainer, especially on their characteristics in terms of social structure; according to this, the average regular participator is male, beyond fifty years of age, well educated, middle class and, apart from all this, a definite party identifier. See Linder 1994, p. 96; Möckli 1994, p. 215f.

11 The Swiss VOX Analysen started only in 1993 to consider systematically the group allegiances of voters and abstainers. Since then findings tend to show that a referendum inititated by, say, the unions does not only mobilise union members but also members of business associations (according to information given by Hans Hirter, Institute of Political Science, University of Berne, 27 March 1997).

is markedly less on one side than on the other, the reason for this is that preferences on that same side are less intense. *If indeed* we can trust that participation in referenda on political issues reflects the existence and the intensity of the preferences thereon, then the optional referendum is without any further prerequisites the exact means – and the only one – for a sectoral unit as a whole to express themselves politically: it includes the organised, the *ad hoc* members, those who 'share the risks', and excludes only those who do not bother.

All problems of definition and distinction notwithstanding, the veto rights of sectoral units will, contrary to those of the regional units, (in principle, at least) tend to embrace a wide range of decisions. There are no specific spheres of autonomy to safeguard which might suggest limiting these vetoes to cases of the infringement of them. Since the core interests of sectoral minorities liable to be violated by European decisions are too unspecific to be identified and classified beforehand, this veto will in fact have to operate in the way of an unqualified, 'normal' optional referendum. It will have to be applicable against any sectoral regulation, including 'regulations to end regulation'. With so comprehensive a means of blockage, its procedures will have to be devised the more carefully.

Procedures

Of the many proposals submitted before the IGC 1996/97, very few advocated any direct-democratic instrument. The rare examples are the Austrian and Italian governments and the group Eurotopia; the Reflection Group briefly discussed but rejected the idea. Likewise, only a few authors have as yet dealt with referenda.[12] Unfortunately, most of those who do so remain exceedingly vague and do not debate details and procedures (one of the rare exceptions here is Nentwich (1998) who suggests a whole bunch of direct-democratic instruments). Moreover, reference is made to Europe-wide referenda only, not to minority rights. So there is little to rely on in this respect, which is one of the

12 It has to be noted though that after the referenda on the Maastricht Treaty direct-democratic instruments met with more interest than usual. See Bohnet & Frey 1994; Opp 1994; Zürn 1996; Grande 1996a; Erne et al. 1995; Nentwich 1998; Held 1991 (who, to my knowledge, is the only one to allude to something nearing a sectoral veto; see p. 233).

reasons why the following suggestions will be of a rather tentative and preliminary nature: they are submitted for further debate. I shall undertake to find 'first answers' to the questions of (1) in what ways veto rights and popular initiatives differ and what procedural consequences to draw from this; (2) to whom to assign the right to set in motion any of the referenda; (3) which majorities and which quora to request in which cases; (4) what immediate effects the referenda ought to have; and (5) to which types of decisions they are to be applied. Finally (6) the need for a mandatory referendum on matters of a quasi-constitutional nature will have to be considered.

Vetoes and initiatives

The Austrian-Italian move just mentioned suggested including in Art. 8e TEC the right of European citizens to petition some new act or other to be passed by the EP (which then should proceed in accordance with Art. 138b).[13] I, on the other hand, have so far dealt with direct-democratic veto rights only. Vetoes and 'popular initiatives'[14] are two different kettles of fish with different effects and hence call for different procedures. The usual view is (1) that of 'braking' referenda (i.e., vetoes) and 'innovating' initiatives (Linder 1994, p. 100ff.), as well as (2) that of the veto being the instrument of organised interests (and other minorities) and the initiative one of 'social movements', new *ad hoc* groups, or more or less of the active citizen. Accordingly, the veto tends to be harshly censured as blocking progress, even as an obstacle to democracy, and the initiative praised as the appropriate means to render an otherwise representative democracy more responsive – not only to people's wishes but, more specifically, to new problems arising within society. Matters are not, however, quite so simple as this. A number of examples might be given where things were just the other way round: with initiatives used as an attempt to impose a narrow interest on a baffled society and the veto as the only means to bring home to politicians how far they had deviated from the preferences even of majorities.

13 This implies that the proposed device is in fact intended to be no more than a rather weak means of agenda setting by the people; for according to Art. 138 b the EP may only 'request the Commission to submit any appropriate proposal' on the respective subject matter.
14 What is meant here by 'popular initiative' is the popular vote following up the 'public petition' (demanding a new act or policy), finally to decide the matter by the people.

The different logic of both instruments – whether in the hands of organised interests or of wider and (perhaps) more unspecific movements – is that of defending old rights (entrenched by law or by habit), on the one hand, and of demanding some new policy (which may be of any kind: regulative, protective, redistributive), on the other. One is the means to protect minorities against inconsiderate majorities, while the other requests of the political élite to alter its policies and adopt new ones. Such new policies, however, ought not to be those that benefit minorities only. The procedures of the two direct-democratic devices should differ accordingly: both the quorum to set in motion the popular vote and the amount of votes required for the latter's success should be higher in case of the popular initiative. Especially in the European context, where a public in the strict sense is lacking and where, instead, various interest groups compete more or less unobservedly to obtain subsidies and privileges by legal and sometimes even illegal means, it is debatable whether for the time being public petitions should be allowed to be decided by a popular vote at all or whether the respective matter should not be left – as one of first priority – to the legislative institutions.[15] Things are different where rights or even the autonomy of minorities are defended. For the veto to become effective, it should in principle suffice that the respective unit more or less unanimously subscribes to it.

Who may initiate?

If vetoes are a means of protecting minority rights, whoever initiates them should make unequivocally clear that they are rightfully speaking for such a minority. In the case of the regional veto this stipulation will present few problems. In principle, anybody in one of those regions defending their autonomy would be entitled to set it in motion, provided he is supported in this by an adequate proportion of this region's electorate. Since these differ in size, it would be unwise to fix an absolute number as quorum; 'ten per cent of the electorate', on the other hand, sounds a pretty stiff requirement, considering the nearly 18 million population and 13 million electorate

15 Nentwich (1998) suggests that a referendum should be held only when EP and Council fail to enact the proposed policy. According to his proposal, the petition alone would have to meet the requirement of 3 or 4 per cent of the European electorate and the same portion of voters in at least five of the member states (compared with a tenth at least of the electorate of at least three member states, in the Austrian-Italian move); it does not say anything about the required majority in the referendum proper.

of Northrhine-Westfalia. My suggestion would be to settle for something midway and ask for a quorum of 5 per cent of the electorate, but not more than 100,000 signatures. Apart from this, the regional parliament or a part of it – albeit not the government – should be entitled to call for such a direct-democratic veto.

It is much more difficult to define quora to set the optional referendum going because of the unknown size of the presupposed sectoral units. In a first experimental stage it would seem to be advisable to leave the petitioning to organised groups (or considerable parts of them), provided it is the combined effort of organisations of (or based in) at least two member countries, or to NGOs which operate transnationally anyway. Such a course recommends itself the more since at present citizens are little likely to associate and form *ad hoc* groups across boundaries. It should, however, not be precluded that *ad hoc* groups, if they do come into being, be granted the right of initiative. In most cases those groups' 'sectoral quality' will be self-evident. Yet it might be wise to have it ascertained by some sort of (impartial) electoral commission, possibly attached to the ECJ but not composed of judges. I am aware that the composition of such a body will meet with some problems: it will not be an easy task to safeguard its impartiality.

Once initiated, the petition for an optional referendum should have to meet a quorum that is comparatively small, especially since it is hardly possible to define it in proportionate terms. Again, the stipulation should be that citizens in at least two member countries subscribe to make the move successful; as a starting-point, I should suggest a quorum of 50,000 in each of them.

Majorities required

If a popular initiative – that is, a popular vote demanding a new policy to be enacted – were to be installed, it should (as has been argued above) come near a real majority in Europe to win its point: a majority of the European electorate ought to participate and a majority of those give their consent. It might even be sensible to add the further requirement of what the Swiss call the *Ständemehr*, i.e., the consent of citizens in a *majority of countries*.[16] As for the veto, the requirement of Europe-wide majorities would immediately destroy its character of protection of minority rights. In nation-states this latter object does present some thorny legitimatory problems, for the – howsoever justified – claim of

16 This would be a special case of 'concurrent majorities'.

minorities to have their rights safeguarded stands against the equally legitimate claim of the national majority not to have their interests thwarted; hence a fine balance between the two claims will have to be struck. In Europe the situation is different in so far as European decisions, prepared in issue networks and legally enacted by Council and EP, do not represent the will of a genuine 'European majority' but are compromises between various minorities at best and benefit single minorities at worst. So the question here is one of protecting minorities against minorities and of making the whole business more visible and transparent.

Yet in order to offer proof that the matter at hand touches its core interests or entrenched rights, the respective minority should be obliged to demonstrate (where possible) that most of its members can in fact be roused over the issue. In the case of the regional veto this implies that it ought to be backed by a majority of its own electorate at least, with a majority of them actually casting their vote. The qualified majority should be followed up by a second referendum, this time in the member-state of which the region is a component unit, in case the member state's authorities were contradicting the region's claims; in this second ballot a simple majority of participants should suffice. These requirements given, abstention alone would defeat the veto in the first referendum: those not backing it could simply stay at home. In the second referendum those who are opposed to the region's veto would also have to cast their vote in order to make it fail. Governments, that is, would be forced to offer some very good arguments to induce the electorate to feel as strongly about the matter as the region's citizens do (who, incidentally, may well be supported by citizens of the other regions of the member state). If, however, the latter had been nearly unanimously opposed to the loss of competence in question – a fact to be expressed by a majority of two-thirds backing the veto in the first referendum – no second ballot ought to be required.

The minorities to be protected by the sectoral veto will rather frequently turn out to be majorities: of consumers, for instance, or of sharers of environmental risks. It will, however, not normally be known beforehand whether this will be the case. Above, the sectoral unit was (tentatively) defined by the shared interests or shared risks, the awareness of those, and the readiness to act accordingly. The reverse side of this argument is that those citizens who abstain from the popular vote, even if by objective criteria they belong to the respective sector, do not possess preferences intense enough really to be bothered. This is why I suggest in such cases considering the simple majority of participants as sufficient for the success of the referendum – provided the participants originate from at least three member countries. In the referendum proper, that is, the cross-national character of the sectoral unit should be made even more visible than in the petition to set it going. The requirement does not mean, of course, that ballot boxes are to be put up in three member countries only. Citizens in all member countries should be allowed (and given opportunity) to cast their vote.[17]

Although it is logically not quite consistent with the unanimity principle, a kind of negligibility threshold recommends itself for the optional referendum for practical reasons. I propose to set this at around 10 per cent at least of the combined electorates if indeed not more than three countries are involved – and at 2 or 3 per cent at least in each of them – and lower if they are more. Such requirements appear advisable, too, to prevent the sectoral veto from being (mis)used as a guise for the veto of powerful *national* interest groups. It should by all means be made impossible that (for instance) German or French farmers by dint of 'buying' a few votes in, say, Luxemburg and Denmark, may win their point and block a reform of the Common Agricultural Policy.

The Effects

The effect of the veto cannot be any other than the blockage of the EU policy thus challenged. Whenever some regional unit had successfully applied its veto against a particular policy, the result could not be – as is the case now (sometimes) with the member states' vetoes – the region's 'opting out'; in the case of the sectoral veto opt-outs are not feasible, anyhow. Instead, the policy in question would not be adopted at Community level but dealt with separately by the member states or their subunits, no matter which issue it was. This implies at the same time that one region's veto would not at all thwart any other minority's interests. Nobody would be forced to do anything that he did not wish; there would only be put a brake on compulsory 'harmonisation'.

The blockage would be a highly effective one; for, contrary to the veto in the Council, it could not be overcome by package-deals (or only in the longer run, by subsequent 'two level' negotiations,

---

17 Which implies, for practical reasons, that votes are cast by letter or by electronic means.

including those units or groups whose core interests had been offended). By its own logic, the veto will thus inevitably possess a definite bias against EU regulation. This bias is, however, not identical with one against regulation as such. Since European harmonisation frequently takes the shape of abolishing member-state regulations, the blocking referenda could – only on the face of it paradoxically – well be votes for the 'active state(s)'.

It should go without saying that the European citizens' veto would for the time being be the 'last word' in the respective matter. It particularly precludes the ECJ's power to annul the 'people's choice' on the grounds that it was not in line with the treaty and its teleology.

Types of Decisions

With instruments that can effectively block European policy making, the question arises whether their application ought not be restricted to very few decisions only. In fact I have made clear from the outset that the regional veto should, in principle, be applied solely to decisions concerning the assignment of competences, and only to those which actually threaten to lead to a loss of the regions' own competences. European practice has, however, been one of clandestine expansion of Community powers; and in the absence of a catalogue of competences it is difficult anyhow to identify clearly those decisions which alter the distribution of powers. Decisions are normally on policies which in their turn may or may not have that effect. Hence, although the principle – decisions on competences only – may be clear-cut and restrictive, the practice is probably not. The proposed recall of competences will complicate the matter even further, for any 'normal', day-to-day policy decision can lead to the sudden realisation, on the part of a region, that one of its powers of jurisdiction may irretrievably have been lost. For the time being the regional veto would inevitably be one against European policy decisions, whatever their foundation in treaty norms or in the logic of things. The only stipulation will be that the initiators are held to justify somewhat plausibly that the challenged decision seriously violates one or other of their entrenched rights. Assuming that these rights are rather unambiguously circumscribed in the regions' own 'constitutional contracts', the matter will be much more clear-cut from their angle than from that of the European institutions; hence the burden of proof would have to rest on the regions. One may cherish hopes, though, that the veto's sheer existence will act as a spur on Euro-politicians (and on the Commission, especially) to sort out the existing muddle and to render the distribution of competences more transparent – if only with the object of reducing the number of possible vetoes.

Even now there will be no need, however, for a special agency to pass verdicts on petitioned regional vetoes as being indeed within the realm of the assignment of powers. Any regional actor petitioning for the veto would himself have to convince his voters that the question at hand was one of the loss of crucial regional powers. Since it can be assumed that the regional electorate disagrees as much over policy issues as it is united over the matter of regional identity and autonomy, he will have to have some very good arguments to mobilise the required majorities.

For the proposed optional referendum no restriction suggests itself – none other, that is, than the general one that referenda (if avoidable) should not be applied to any decision of the redistributive kind.

The veto rights dealt with so far will mainly be applied to Community legislation, i.e., to its secondary law. Measures of primary law, or quasi-constitutional acts, may require different treatment and will be dealt with subsequently.

A Mandatory Referendum

The main thrust of my argument (and of the proposal derived from this) is to grant participatory rights to non-national, i.e., to subnational and to cross-national units, in order to adapt the principle of democratic legitimisation of decision-making to the multi-layer and multi-dimensional character of European politics. The object of rendering the latter democratic will, however, require at crucial stages in the further development of the European polity that not only regional and sectoral minorities have the right to contradict but the European public in their entirety be asked their consent. According to the basic contractarian principle, every new contractual step – additional treaty or treaty revision – should be submitted to the European citizens for approval or rejection. The proposed system of veto rights, that is, ought to be complemented by a Europe-wide mandatory referendum on all matters of a quasi-constitutional nature.

Mandatory referenda might also be considered useful whenever Council and EP disagree over European legislation. But preferably this instrument ought to be reserved to matters of EU primary law, the legitimisation of which until now is exclusively left to the discretion of the member states. Foreseeably, primary law will henceforth develop in two different ways: there will be treaty revisions concerning the community as a whole (which will be mainly of an institutional kind; case 1), and there will be the cases of 'variable geometry' in which only parts of the membership have an interest (case 2). The mandatory referendum will have to adapt to these two basically different situations, hence it has to occur in two different versions.

Since it is obligatory, this referendum does not need specific initiating procedures, of course. As for the majorities necessary, to signal European citizens' consent to the issue(s) of primary law in question, an overall European majority – whether of votes cast or absolute – cannot suffice, if we want to stick to contractarian principles. Instead, a majority of votes cast in all member countries is required in case 1. This is a somewhat steeper hurdle for the ratification of treaty revisions than that of the 'concurrent majorities' suggested by some other authors, combining the overall European majority with majorities in the majority of countries (cf. the Swiss *Ständemehr*). In case 2, it might reasonably be suggested holding the referendum only in those countries which actually want to be parties to the specific contract (like the 'Schengen-agreements', for instance). Such a limitation would not do, however, considering the claim to facilitate the democratic control of the passing of European primary law *Europe-wide*. If this demand is to be obeyed, citizens in all member countries ought to be given the opportunity to voice their assent or dissent to the contract at hand, no matter whether their governments have decided to join in or not. It is at least conceivable that citizens do not always share their governments' stance and are inclined to disavow them if given the chance. In defining the majorities prescribed for such an 'opting in' it would be inadequate to think in terms of 'negligibility thresholds'. It needs to be emphasised once more that the matter at stake is not one of protecting minority interests, but of a majority reasserting itself. Hence one would be well advised to call for an absolute majority – i.e., not just the majority of the votes cast, but a majority of the respective country's electorate in any such case.

The effect of the mandatory referendum would in case 1 be the blockage of the contractual step at hand if it does not find the approval of the majority of all the European *demoi*, counted by national units. Although Europe-wide by legal status, this variant of the mandatory referendum would therefore amount to a direct-democratic version of the member-state veto. One should bear in mind, though, that the popular vote might well make a government's veto in the Council invalid, occasionally. Opt-outs ought to be precluded in case 1 since the latter by definition is one of matters of 'common concern'. In case 2, the referendum's effect would be a trifle more complex for here the *demoi* would decide both on the content of the specific contract and on the question of who are to be the parties to it: in fact they would determine the shape the 'variable geometry' is going to take. 'Opt-ins' could not, however, be automatically effected; instead, such an outcome of one or other of the national referenda would mostly result in renewed negotiations.

This does not only sound rather complicated: it will certainly be even more so in practice. And although various other authors have suggested a mandatory 'constitutional' referendum in recent years, I judge it of all direct-democratic instruments the least likely to be acceptable to member states as well as to European institutions – at any rate in the shape sketched here which, however, seems to be the only one to meet the requirements demanded by contractualism. This is one of the reasons why I have hesitated to include the mandatory referendum in my proposal (see above, p. 103 f.). The other grievance is that a mandatory referendum which is held nation-wide (albeit on the basis of European citizenship) and is in actual fact clearly referring to national European policies, might clash with some of the member states' basic constitutional principles and hence cause a new incompatibility problem.[18] Something of the sort ought to be considered though – a 'lean version' of the proposed device, perhaps – if the further constitutional development in Europe is to be properly legitimised.

Some Illustrations

Two examples, one wholly fictitious (at the moment), the other one more within the realms of possibility, may serve to illustrate the way in which the direct-democratic vetoes can work.

(1) The Territorial Veto

One of the few remnants of the German *Länders'* sovereignty is what is called their 'cultural sovereignty' (*Kulturhoheit*): their right to have

---

18 In contrast, the direct-democratic vetoes of regional and sectoral units do not cause such problems, since they are subnational in character and refer unequivocally to European (secondary) law.

it their own way in all matters of culture (including broadcasting), religion, and education. With hardly any other sphere of autonomy left to them, some of the *Länder* defend this particular bit rather jealously against infringements of any kind. Now, in Art. 126, the EC Treaty constitutes a community competence in exactly this policy area: in educational policy. Feeling obliged by statutes as well as by the treaty's inherent teleology to promote the 'ever closer union' of the EU's peoples, the Commission might some day consider compulsory religious instruction in state schools, especially when in the care of the churches themselves (as is the practice in all but two of the German *Länder*[19]), as a serious impediment to the 'free flow of persons' and might propose a regulation aiming at putting an end to this practice. The EP, also bent on the promotion of integration and harmonisation, could be expected to assent, some grumbling coming from German and Irish MEPs notwithstanding; in the Council Germany might be induced by some package-deal or other to keep a low profile.

The regulation thus issued would, of course, have direct effect down to the smallest Bavarian village school and would encourage agnostic parents to try to enforce it via the courts. Bavaria, however, is the one *Land* which is most emphatically bent on having its own educational policy, and even more so on having the privileges of the churches protected. The instrument of the territorial veto given, it does not require much fantasy to imagine Bavarian CSU politicians eagerly grasping it.[20] A major part of the Bavarian parliament could be expected to petition a veto against the EU assuming a competence in school matters, on the grounds that it is an infringement of the German *Länders'* 'cultural sovereignty'.

Nor do we have to strain our powers of imagination to expect the petition to meet the requirement of 10 per cent of the Bavarian electorate subscribing without any great difficulty; consequently a referendum would have to be held on the matter in Bavaria (first referendum). Let us assume that this could mobilise 57 per cent of the voters, with most of them endorsing the veto. Then a second referendum would have to follow in the Federal Republic as a whole, the outcome of which would be much more unpredictable. Maybe most non-Bavarians (and agnostics) would not really bother

19 This specific feature of German educational policy is protected not only by the *Kulturhoheit* of the *Länder* but also by Art. 7 Par. 2 and 3 of the Basic Law which constitutes a basic right of Germans known as *Elternrecht* – i.e., the right of parents to have their children instructed in religion at normal schools.

20 The Bavarian constitution allows popular petitions and popular votes of old. In 1995 these instruments were introduced into local politics, too. The Bavarian 'state party', the CSU, rather cleverly knows how to make use of them for its own ends.

and hence abstain, a not altogether unlikely result if one takes into account that the federal government of which the Bavarian CSU forms a part must be rather embarrassed and unable to campaign wholeheartedly against the veto. Thus the Bavarians (supported, however, by a number of devout Catholics and staunch federalists) might win their point with only 27 per cent of the German electorate participating (case I). On the other hand, many non-Bavarians might still be furious about the Bavarians' behaviour in the 'Crucifix affair',[21] or altogether exasperated with Bavarian eccentricities, and let themselves be roused to go to the polls. With the high turnout of 53 per cent of the German electorate the veto would very probably be rejected (case II). Yet a third possibility is that Bavarians feel so strongly on the issue that they oppose the EU regulation nearly unanimously. Case III, that is, might be that of about 80 per cent of their electorate participating in the first referendum and a majority of 77 per cent of those endorsing the veto, a result which would render the second ballot superfluous.

In case II the EU could go ahead with its harmonising policy. But both in case I and III not only the EU regulation concerning religious instruction in schools would be invalidated. Rather, the European institutions would for the time being be stopped from meddling with the member states' educational policies. This would, however, not hinder any other member-state government (or parliament) to proceed in accordance with the rejected regulation's intentions.

(2) The Sectoral Veto

For several years now a fierce battle has been fought in Brussels and Strassburg over the 'Novel Food' regulation proposed by the Commission in November 1993 (to revise or replace some older ones, issued since 1990).[22] The proposal did not just aim at

---

21 In 1995 the German Constitutional Court tried to enforce agnostic parents' right to object to a crucifix hanging on the wall of every schoolroom their children sat in (as is the habit in every Bavarian school). The ruling caused an uproar in Bavaria, much mud was thrown on the Court; and an Act was prepared which to the better part attempts to revoke the verdict.

22 In the early 1990s the Commission had already issued a proposal for a directive on the same subject. Both directives and regulations on this and related subjects have in fact existed. Their (respective) revision has been a matter of constant debate; and stances on them appear to have changed frequently. As a whole, the history of European legislation on 'Novel Food' is a fine example of the maze the interested European citizen enters once he or she wants to find out in detail what the actual legal situation with regard to specific issues is: it is extremely difficult not to lose the thread. Nor has the history of the novel food issue come to its end yet. New proposals have already been issued.

harmonising member countries' policies concerning the release of genetically-modified organisms (GMO) and the marketing of food containing or consisting of GMOs, but more particularly at forcing all member countries to accept such food as 'normal' and not to be distinguished from other food. Instead of intending to harmonise policies of consumer protection, the primary object was explicitly to remove 'actual or potential barriers to trade', in the interest of food industries. The major bone of contention in the matter, even before the Commission's proposal had been submitted, was the question of comprehensive as well as compulsory labelling of the 'novel food' as containing GMOs, and whether member states would have the right to demand such labelling of producers unilaterally (which was what some of the older rules had envisaged). The draft proposal of 1993 flatly denied member states this right as being incompatible with the concept of the single market.

In 1995 and in subsequent years, the co-decision procedure was put to the test over the issue. The Commission proposal was supported by the Council but met with some grave doubts in the first reading in the EP. Following the procedure laid down in Art. 189 b TEC, the Council then adopted a 'common position' which considered some of these doubts but rejected most of them; in this, the Council acted by qualified majority: the common position was opposed by Austrians, Danes, Germans and Swedes. In March 1996 the EP had to deal with the common position. Although a majority of MEPs was still in favour of a comprehensive labelling, the opponents of the regulation did not meet the requirement needed for the rejection of a common position, which is the 'absolute majority of component members'. With its absolute majority the EP did, however, vote for an amendment in the shape of a restricted version of labelling, thus trying to find a compromise between the positions of Commission and Council (and industry) on the one hand and MEPs (Socialists and Greens, mostly) and consumer protectors on the other. The Council majority did not relish the compromise and rejected the amendments proposed by the EP in the next step (in July 1996);[23] hence the matter was put before the Conciliation Committee which had then the task of finding 'a compromise between various compromises', a process

---

23 Interestingly enough, the opponents were others than those who had opposed the common position before; in a manner of speaking, there was a 'negative' coalition now between those who wanted no labelling at all and those who considered the restricted version of labelling novel food insufficient.

which lasted until early in 1997.[24] The modified regulation was finally approved by the EP in March 1997 and came into force in all member countries in May. In response to growing concern by the public, however, the Commission was in April 1997 already drafting new proposals which envisage more extensive labelling of raw materials but which are (according to Greenpeace and other opponents) still far from demanding strict and comprehensive labelling of food. So the issue will stay with us for some time.

The various steps of European decision-making normally take place in a sphere wholly remote from the European peoples. But meanwhile the *demos* itself has entered the stage where the novel food drama is enacted. On 15 April 1997 about 1.2 million Austrians (which is more than 21 per cent of the Austrian electorate) subscribed a public petition demanding an act which bans the production of genetically-modified food as well as the release of GMOs in Austria. The petition includes the demand to ban imports of genetically-altered maize, implicitly requesting the government to pursue the case if needed through all the courts up to the ECJ. Furthermore, the petition can be read as a plea for the comprehensive and compulsory labelling of food containing GMOs in Austria, irrespective of what the rest of Europe does. The question now is how the European institutions will react to such a policy if it is indeed implemented – a policy clearly at odds with European law and a definite impediment to the free flow of goods in Europe but based on the explicit will of the people. The responsible commissioner Mr Bangemann's immediate reaction to the Austrian petition was a somewhat resigned one: 'If the majority wishes it, we will do so', referring to the compulsory labelling of novel food, although he confessed himself to be still opposed to it, personally. At the same time his colleague Ritt Bjerregaard (responsible for the environment) is already drafting the above-mentioned new proposals. This yielding attitude does, however, not preclude (for instance) the ECJ's insistence on Austria's applying the European rules to the letter (as long as these are valid); nor is it at all certain that the express wish of the Austrian electorate will impress the majority in the Council.

If a sectoral veto was already in existence, the case would be a quite straightforward one. The Austrian consumer associations,

24 At the same time the EP and Council agreed upon a regulation (following the proposal originally issued in July 1992) which concedes that with some products and in some countries a comprehensive information for consumers might be required, but which leaves the decision on details to 'comitology'.

combined with (say) their Danish colleagues and/or Greenpeace, could have (even in the same ballot with their Austrian public petition) petitioned an optional referendum against the Novel Food regulation; as things stand, they would have found no difficulty at all in meeting the required quorum of subscribers in both countries. Participation in the subsequent referendum might not be over-impressive, as regards percentages of the European population. Citizens in the Mediterranean countries would plainly be uninterested, as would probably be those in France and Britain. The veto could be successful all the same, provided that the required quorum of 10 per cent of the electorate of three countries at least participate. With a turnout of (say) 43 per cent Austria, 42 per cent in Denmark, 39 per cent in Sweden, 40 per cent in Germany and 13 per cent even in the Netherlands (where farmers are just starting to 're-naturate' their vegetables) the outcome would be way above the 'negligibility threshold', although the turnouts in those countries would add up to a mere 9.6 per cent of the EU's electorate.[25] Understandably, those roused to go to the polls would be only those who feel strongly about the matter, that is those who fear somehow to be threatened by the novel food, on the one hand, and those who fear for their jobs in the food industry, or for Europe's position in the global economy, on the other. Consumers' fears proving to be the stronger ones in this case, we may assume a great majority, nearing two-thirds of participants, to endorse the veto. Such an outcome would only then be unlikely if the electorates of countries participated where the food industry was a major economic factor and where the latter's workers formed a recognisable part of the population.

With the success of the veto, the EC regulation would be invalid, no matter how the European institutions react. As an effect, all member countries (and not only those whose people had participated in the referendum) would be free to label genetically-modified products – or even to ban them altogether – as their respective electorates wish.[26]

25 Supposing that only 28 per cent of the German electorate went to the polls, European turnout would go down to 7.5 per cent. The example illustrates how difficult it will be to meet any requirements defined 'Europe-wide'. Even the apparently modest quorum of 10 per cent of the all-European electorate will hardly be achieved when participation in the large countries remains negligible.
26 Depending on how narrowly the subject matter of the referendum had been defined, they would, however, be free to do so only within the bounds of the (above-mentioned, see footnote 108) numerous EC rules on 'related subjects' which might not have been invalidated by the veto.

The Mandatory Referendum

'Maastricht II' and EMU may serve to illustrate how the mandatory referendum could work. Had the IGC in Amsterdam agreed upon a substantial strengthening of the EP and the abolition of the veto in the Council – which it has not, of course – these decisions should have been subjected to the approval of the European electorate. Altering rules of decision-making at European level, the matter would clearly have been one of 'common concern' (i.e., an example of 'case 1' as defined above); hence not only a Europe-wide majority would have been required for ratification but a majority of votes cast in all member countries. Suppose that the first requirement had been met in the referendum, but the voters both of Britain and of France had withheld their consent (albeit with a low turnout, indicating that the preferences of Eurosceptics are more intense than those of sympathisers). As a result, the treaty revision agreed upon by the IGC could not come into force.

At the next summit, the participants of the EMU's first stage will be determined – say, the Benelux countries, Germany, France, and Spain (case 2). The electorates of the respective countries would then be called to the ballot box to assent to the replacement of their currency by the Euro;[27] but voters in other member countries would also be given the opportunity to participate in the referendum. A not wholly unsurprising outcome might be that in five of the six countries which are immediately concerned voters would approve of joining the EMU; but those of Germany would not. On the other hand, a sufficient part of the Danish and Italian electorate would participate, requiring with convincing majorities their respective countries to be one of the party. This result would clearly be awkward for governments and negotiators and probably be followed up by rather hectic activities. Since Italy had, in 1997, missed in part the convergence criteria fixed by 'Maastricht I', the Italian vote could not enable Italy to join immediately but would enforce renewed and somewhat pressing negotiations between Italy, EMU countries and the European Monetary Institute. In the case of Denmark its government would be obliged to enter into negotiations which it had so far avoided. A popular vote (of sufficient proportion) in Sweden might cause some embarrassment too, no matter what its outcome. If positive it would disavow the

---

27 Incidentally, according to the system of veto rights proposed here, the Euro could not be stopped by way of the territorial or the sectoral veto. Currency matters are clearly not in the competence of regional subunits but matters of national policy; nor can they in any way be defined as 'sectoral'.

Swedish government which wants to remain outside the EMU; if negative it would cause some headaches in the Council whose members think themselves entitled to decide with their majority about the countries which are to participate as long as they have not formally opted out at the right moment (i.e., when the Maastricht Treaty was agreed upon).

Apart from the more or less immediate effects, these referenda and their disturbing results might teach European actors a lesson which could prove decisive for the further development of the European polity. Hopefully, the different outcomes of case 1 and case 2 referenda would induce actors and intergovernmental negotiators to proceed more cautiously with Europe-wide regulations and to apply equal care to matters of institutional reform. In the example introduced here, negotiators would (provided they act rationally) in the next step make an attempt to differentiate decision-making procedures according to members and sectors affected. 'Strengthening the EP' would then in the next draft – as far as its plenum (representing the entirety of EU members) is concerned – be strictly limited to a very narrow range of policy areas and types of decisions. Likewise, majority voting in the Council as a whole would be restricted to a narrow range of areas, but might be accepted as common practice between those members which are united in a specific measure of extra-integration (like EMU, or the Schengen agreements). In the long run, the need to secure popular consent for both types of politics would induce actors to find and invent means to give an institutional form to the 'variable geometry' of European politics. It might even lead to their appreciation of devices such as the optional (sectoral) referendum.

A Summary Of The Proposal

What I propose here is (1) to complement the existing institutions and procedures of EU decision-making by direct-democratic instruments, mainly in the shape of vetoes against decisions reached in the existing set-up.

(2) The first of these is the veto of regional units which possess autonomous status and are materially threatened in their status by a European integration that acknowledges states and their rights but does not register the rights of the states' component units. The regional veto shall be applicable to any decision touching on the

latter's spheres of autonomy (but *only* to such decisions), and ought to be accepted as a blockage if backed fairly unanimously by the unit's citizens. Below a threshold indicating near-unanimity the regional veto should be finally decided upon in a second referendum, this time nation-wide in the respective country: forcing its majority to think twice about the matter, and demonstrating whether or not the respective European legislation is backed by a majority in that country, at all.

(3) The second instrument is a sectoral veto, invented with the aim of rendering the dealings of European policy networks more transparent and holding them accountable to their particular constituencies. Because of the (theoretical as well as practical) difficulty of identifying such units (and their sizes) beforehand, this veto will have to take the shape of an optional referendum, to be decided by a simple majority of participators, provided that this majority is in fact cross-national (i.e., combining sufficient parts of the electorates of at least three member countries).

(4) Both these vetoes are meant to result not in opt-outs but to effectively block the respective policies at European level. Inevitably, this implies a reassertion of nation-state competences for the time being since any competence denied the European level falls back to that of member states, in the first place.

(5) In order to heighten the responsiveness of European policy making, the instrument of public petition, demanding specific acts or policies to be set on the European agenda, may be added to the system of veto rights. I am, however, sceptical about the advisability of having such initiatives finally decided by popular votes, too. At any rate, much greater majorities will be required in this case than in that of the vetoes.

(6) Any new contracts and quasi-constitutional steps ought to be approved by the European *demoi* in a mandatory referendum. In the absence of a European *demos* (in the singular), this would in the case of matters of common concern (i.e., mainly institutional reform) require the consent of majorities in all member countries, hence amount to a direct-democratic veto of member states. In the case of contracts involving only part of the membership, voters in all member countries should nonetheless be given the opportunity to participate in the referendum to legitimise both the decision to join and that to opt out.

6

MAJOR OBJECTIONS

Democratic Ambivalence
(Or: How Democratic Is Democracy?)

Some Advantages Of The Proposal

The proposed system of direct-democratic veto rights can be expected to meet most of the requirements listed above. Contrary to parliamentary institutions (to be strengthened or altered), further transnational committees, or additional chambers of whatever kind, this device has the advantages (1) of *not* being *statist*, in neither presupposing a state-like development nor itself being a first step in this direction; and (2) of allowing for a high degree of *flexibility* instead, as regards the further completion of the union (in whatever respects), its 'variable geometries', and the multi-dimensionality of European policy making. Whereas parliamentary institutions invariably tend to strengthen the centre of a composite polity and are therefore prone to violate some or other of the constitutional principles of the component units, the proposed veto rights are (3) *compatible* with the members' (democratic) political systems in so far as they are unlikely to alter the ways they normally operate. While safeguarding the rights of the federations' units, they would not materially harm, for instance, a member state's parliamentary system since they would not be applied at national but only at European level.[1] In fact they might even restore these systems to their old strength by recapturing the lost room of manoeuvre for parliamentary control; for a petition for a referendum would provide MPs with all the justification they at present seem to lack, to inspect their

---

1 'At worst', they might act as a sort of leverage at national level, rendering political institutions more responsive to people's preferences. This, however, cannot seriously be considered a drawback.

governments' European policies more closely. In short: rights (of autonomy and/or participation) which up to now are in danger of being sacrificed to the process of integration will have a fair chance of survival.

In establishing the compatibility which has so far been lacking, the proposed device seems to be (4) one of the few conceivable ways of holding governance in a 'union of old nations' *accountable*, at its various levels: governments or authorities at neither level will be able – as they are now – to hide one behind the other, blurring responsibilities. In the public debates preceding the referenda the share of any of them in the bargains or compromises thus challenged will inevitably be laid open. In this way, the direct-democratic vetoes will at the same time (5) enhance the *transparency* of European politics: of politics that are, in essence, those of bargaining systems. Again, the proposed device appears to be one of the very few conceivable answers to the puzzle of how to achieve a modicum of democratic control and responsiveness in politics as opaque as network politics are. Since participation in them is by necessity limited they need ways of opening up which cannot be gained by any representative mode, for every representative added to the bargaining network would himself immediately be a part (or 'node') of it and thus unfit for the control which is required in the interests of those represented.

(6) Composite polities which are characterised by the 'radical *diversity*' of their people(s) cannot be democratised nor be made responsive to their citizens' preferences by any device relying on majority rule. There is hardly any other way to do this than to combine minority rights and democratic methods: hence referenda benefiting minorities. And (7), last but not least, if the collective *identity* and the quality of *demos* which so far are assumed to be absent among the peoples of Europe do in fact grow with the amount of citizens' rights and the shared experience of using them, then one of the major advantages of the proposed instruments will be the potential they possess of encouraging the growth of a sense of European identity in Europe's *multiple demoi*.

I refrain, at this point, from enlarging upon further advantages the proposal might have in a more theoretical perspective. It might, for instance, be an answer to the problem of lost congruence (of participation in and effects of decisions) in an age of globalisation, as well as to those raised by the 'postmodern' phenomenon of 'disembedding', i.e., the erosion of identifiable collective identities and milieus, and the resulting fluid state of varying, overlapping, intermingling *ad hoc* groups. The preferences of the latter's quasi-members may nonetheless be sufficiently intense to render it by any democratic terms unjustifiable to have them systematically ignored simply because they do not – and could not – be formally organised in the traditional way. Democratic theory has so far found it exceedingly difficult to deal with such developments which simply do not seem to fit the ways and means of representative democracy. Regarding the functional dimension of politics representative devices are doomed to failure when groups and stable allegiances dissolve.

Yet, up to now the 'mainstream' of democratic theory has been as distrustful of most varieties of direct democracy as its new normative versions (sketched above) are. Some authors even go so far as to flatly accuse direct-democratic devices of being inherently *un*democratic. In a way, we end up with the question how democratic democracy is – a question which is less nonsensical than it sounds since it has a lot to do with the way democracy is defined, with the distinction between methods and results, and with the confidence to be placed in the individuals or in a (structured) *demos*. These are, of course, core topics of democratic theory; it would take another book (at least) to discuss them in full. I shall, however, attempt to examine in brief the strength of the main reproaches raised against direct-democratic decision-making.[2]

The Drawbacks Of Direct Democracy

The most common objection is that direct democracy is a threat to liberty and humanity because people are apt to fall an easy prey to populists, demagogues and anti-democrats; if handled in the right way and seized by their prejudices they might vote for anything – for the abolition of minority (and human) rights or democracy itself. A variant to this objection argues that the outcomes of popular votes are a direct result of the money spent in the campaigns preceding them: because the groups with the greatest resources are the most likely to turn popular opinion in their favour, direct democracy would end up in a quasi-legitimate form of unabashed plutocracy. While admitting that there may be some truth in all this one cannot but wonder (a) why people should be expected to be so much more reasonable in selecting persons than in giving their opinion on an issue in which they are interested.

---

2 For a recent discussion of the pros and cons of direct democracy see Budge 1996 (especially chapters 3 and 6); Butler & Ranney 1994 (chapter 2).

After all, as empirical data show, in referenda people are less likely to go to the ballot box from sheer habit or a mere 'sense of duty' than they are in elections. Another question is (b) why citizens should be so much worse, more easily manipulated and led astray by money and bad arguments than their representatives. There is ample evidence that MPs tend to be extremely seducible by money, pliable by leaders, governed by prejudices, not only prey to populists but populist themselves, and in cases even prone to give up democracy and renounce their own rights.[3]

In fact, this kind of criticism, which conservatives have brought forward against representative democracy for ages, is applicable to all versions of democracy. On the other hand, participants in referenda are not quite the fools they are frequently thought to be, nor quite so easily led off the track their own interests – maybe even their reason – indicate them to take. To name but two examples: the Swiss voters have rejected populist initiatives against 'foreign infiltration' already twice;[4] and all the money invested by business in the campaign in favour of joining the 'European Economic Area' (meant to be a halfway-house on the road to the EC) could not induce them to support the scheme. Of course, many commentators have criticised this latter decision as being extremely unwise, unreasonable, and not in accordance with the Swiss people's 'well-understood' interests at all. But that is exactly the material point: *who is to decide upon what is in the interest of citizens, if not they themselves?* And who could rightfully take it upon himself to judge what 'objectively' lies in that interest, against the citizens' expressed will?

Advocates of the latter course would seem to have a lot of explaining to do; and they do have some arguments convincing enough to make their case appear to be a good one, even in democratic terms. For democracy has from the outset been two-faced: it was meant to be a kind of self-government and as such a *method* of arriving at decisions; but to justify the method proof was required that a 'good order' could be achieved this way. The moment the results came in as a criterion to judge upon the quality of political systems the possibly most democratic method soon lost its apparent superiority, and the matter became one of finding a balance between method and results. This is why Rousseau

---

3 Witness, not least, the *Ermächtigungsgesetz* which formally ended the first German parliamentarian democracy.
4 In December 1996 they again rejected a popular initiative against 'illegal immigration'.

invented the figure of the 'legislator'; or why the concept of democracy at a very early stage became so closely linked to the separation of powers; or why from the early liberals up to the present supporters of normative models of democracy so much effort has been spent on devising means of safeguarding the coincidence of democratic decisions with 'reason'.

Public discourse and deliberation are generally considered essential for 'enlightened' and reasonable decision-making. Rational and sensible decisions are not to be arrived at in bargaining processes between interested parties but only in public debate between open-minded individuals capable of yielding to the force of the better argument. This is why disinterestedness has also come to be regarded as a major requirement. Unfortunately, popular votes are decided by interested parties (in fact, this is why they have been invented in the first place); and secondly, they are reproached for lacking the decisive deliberative element: people only decide for or against something, yes or no. The latter criticism, however, is not quite fair because referenda are preceded by campaigns and their issue debated extensively in public; probably much more than any other issue on the political agenda normally is. People may nonetheless be little inclined to give way to better arguments; but so are their representatives, bound by manifestos, influenced by affiliated interests and potent donors, and disciplined by whips. As for the disinterestedness, this sounds a plausible requirement for representatives, at least in so far as they ought not be guided by interests other than those of them whom they represent. The principle is an implausible one though if it is applied to citizens; for if there is any benefit in self-government by the people it is to have their own interests and preferences duly considered. It is exactly for this reason that the various proposed devices which aim at enhancing the participation of citizens, but only of those who are disinterested in the issue at hand – as for instance the 'planning cells' (Dienel 1992) or the 'deliberative opinion polls' (Fishkin 1991) – cannot deny a strong flavour of 'symbolic politics'.

A third criticism to be mentioned and one which is based on empirical findings is the high selectivity of referenda. I have already, above, alluded to the middle-class bias and the higher educational level characterising the average regular voter in countries with some direct-democratic experience. The bias may be expected to weaken considerably – even vanish – whenever the issue is one of particular interest to the worse-off, or to workers in particular. Since such issues tend to be of a redistributive nature, however, the better-offs' higher propensity to vote may indeed turn out to be a drawback, and grant an unfair advantage to those who are advantageously placed in society anyway. The resulting bias in favour of the status quo will have to be considered the more seriously the more frequently referenda are held, and the more nation-wide – or Europe-wide – they are in character. I shall come back to this general bias in some detail later.

Closely related to this criticism is another one: that the referenda put minorities at a disadvantage. While there is something to this, in comparatively homogeneous societies – more precisely: in societies where a compact majority faces one or other marginal or peripheral minority – it cannot be said to apply to societies composed of different cultures and milieus none of which could claim to be a majority itself. The fact that turnout tends to be rather low in optional referenda where these are in frequent use points to 'the' majority being rather uninterested, as a rule, and little inclined to suppress minorities. And indeed, Swiss direct democracy is criticised by insiders for favouring minorities instead of neglecting them, resulting in a disproportionate influence of their respective organisations. Yet this latter reproach is not wholly justified either. There is ample empirical evidence[5] to show that supporters and even members of interest groups do not automatically vote in line with their associations' proposals and quite often disavow them in the popular vote. One may therefore safely conclude that referenda, whatever other weaknesses they may have, have the one strength at least of providing a means of correcting the oligarchical deformations of interest politics, and of reducing the selectivity which results from the organisational bias frequently alluded to above, with regard to network politics. Hence direct-democratic instruments cannot *generally* be assumed to heighten the selectivity of a political system: although the propensities to vote and to abstain are distributed unevenly between the social strata, the selectivity originating from such asymmetry is counterbalanced by the chance which this means provides, to correct the selectivities otherwise inherent in the political system.

Yet is it not undemocratic *per se*, after all, to base a number of policy decisions on the participation of a comparatively small portion of the electorate? This question leads us back to the 'battle of principles' and can in the present context, of course, not be

5 Cf. the VOX analyses which evaluate turnout and results of the referenda in Switzerland.

dealt with in due extent. Suffice it instead to refer to the requirement of congruence: if strictly applied, it does not merely permit, but it demands that on a number of issues not the whole populace but only 'those affected' form the relevant constituency. Whenever the matter at stake is not one of 'generalised support', a high rate of participation cannot seriously constitute a value in itself, not least because a maxim like this would ignore the problem of different intensity of preferences. It is difficult to see on what the intrinsic democratic quality, even superiority, of a decision could be founded in which a lukewarm or uninterested majority outvotes a minority feeling keenly about the issue.[6]

Democracy vs. Efficiency

One of the major topics of the age-old debate on democracy has been the 'democracy-efficiency dilemma': there is a general trade-off, it seems, between the amount of citizens' participation in political decision-making and decision-making efficiency. The dilemma is aggravated in a supranational context in which citizens are confronted with the choice of either 'preserv(ing) the authority of a smaller political unit ... within which they could act more effectively to influence the conduct of their government, even though some important matters might remain beyond the capacity of that government to deal with effectively'; or of 'increas(ing) the capacity of a large political unit to deal more effectively with these matters, even if their ability to influence the government in a democratic fashion were significantly less in the larger unit ... than in the smaller unit' (Dahl 1994, p. 23f.). On the face of it, the direct-democratic veto rights suggested here may be taken as a solution to this dilemma, and even as striking an optimal balance: the larger unit would be allowed to take on responsibility unless there are serious objections, in which case citizen participation would be transferred from the national to the higher level finally to decide upon the assignment of responsibility in the matter at hand. Yet the other side of the coin is that referenda have the effect of introducing additional veto-players into the supranational game; they must therefore be expected to impair both the decision-making efficiency and the 'system-effectiveness' of the larger unit.

6 In his considerations on 'functional democracy' Cole (1970) states as a maxim (thereby defending the right to abstain): 'Many and keen voters are best of all; but few and keen voters are next best. A vast and uninstructed electorate voting on a general and undefined issue is the worst of all.' (p. 116).

Thus a second look may reveal that they are just the opposite of an optimising strategy, in terms of the democracy-efficiency dilemma.[7]

Decision-Making Pathologies

The question to be dealt with here then is whether a direct-democratic veto has in fact the same effect as the 'normal' additional veto-player or the requirement of super-majorities. Both of these can be assumed to be identical in so far as they imply that the additional player, or those actors whose consent is required beyond that of the simple majority, acquire the status of a monopolist who will trade his consent for the highest possible gain and can, in a way, hold the others to ransom. Usually such a situation calls for extra-payments for the extra player, which will be the higher the more urgently his consent is needed. In most cases these will literally take the shape of payments ('pork-barrel' solutions), or, more generally, of 'governmental activity which benefits specific ... groups in a discriminatory fashion and which is financed from general taxation'; for once this particular game has started, every player will trade his support for such projects which, since tax-financed, appear to be 'nearly costless', and will himself hasten to introduce similar demands into the game even if he had not thought of them before (Buchanan & Tullock 1962, p. 143f.). The result is known as 'log-rolling': in the process of winning the consent of all players needed for a decision to become effective the 'log rolls' until each of them has obtained support for his own pet proposal. It is as costly (being skewed towards tax-financed subsidies) as time-consuming; and as inefficient (producing high external costs for all those who are not part of the bargain, and very likely for most of those who are, too) as it is ineffective, in so far as it is liable to prevent adequate solutions to the very problems which first set the process in motion.

However, the process of log-rolling cannot be said to be a specific feature of policy making operating under the rule of super-majority only. It is a way of 'vote-trading' quite common under majority rule as well, any time there is no compact majority. In fact it appears to be the only means of paying due regard to different intensities of preferences in majoritarian decision-making (ibid., p.

---

7 Budge (1996, p. 135ff.) discusses at some length the decision-making ineffiencies theoretically to be expected from popular voting in multi-issue situations. Since the latter condition does not apply to the vetoes suggested here, I shall skip this particular aspect of the democracy-efficiency dilemma.

132f.[8]). One may then safely assume that decision-making pathologies such as log-rolling and pork-barrel solutions are a common trait – and necessarily so – of *any* decision-making system that has (in the longer term and not only periodically) to cope with a high degree of fragmentation and in which majorities are usually formed by coalitions, regardless of whether or not super-majorities are institutionalised. European policy making is indisputably distinguished by both: the lack of a compact majority, hence the need for constant coalition-building, and the need for super-majorities; moreover, these features apply both to its formal and to its informal side. From this we should have to conclude that it is basically inefficient, costly, and ineffective, but if the reasoning so far is correct, unavoidably so.

This coincides in fact with the findings of most empirical studies on European policy making. The reform of the European Structural Funds and the somewhat explosive increase in spending on structural (and regional) policy since 1988, as well as their completion by the Cohesion Fund, are cases in point: first the South European countries had to be bribed into accepting economic liberalisation in the Single Market and then the others had to be bribed into accepting the payments going to the backward regions. The result is that now even the richest countries receive payments because they also have some poorer regions (see Marks 1992, p. 194ff.). All in all, this does in cost-benefit terms not sound a particularly efficient way of spending money, nor an effective one, as regards the (redistributive) object of reducing the disparities in wealth and economic development between member countries. Small wonder then that the implementation of the EU's structural policy is judged by many observers to be a costly failure (see Heinelt 1996); small wonder, too, that the latest reform of the Funds in 1993 did not bring forth any material improvement. Another case in point is, of course, the failure to restructure the Common Agricultural Policy (see Rieger 1996, p. 118ff.) which is not only extremely costly and economically completely irrational, but moreover at odds with the otherwise dominating trend to liberalise and leave matters to market (self-) regulation. More generally, decision-making in the EU can (with Majone 1994, p. 137) be characterised as a two-stage process in which the Commission submits proposals which might arguably increase aggregate welfare – even solve pressing problems – but will typically affect and benefit member states rather differently; hence, in

8 But see Weale (1998) who attempts to prove that such 'pathologies' are untypical of majoritarian decision-making.

a second stage, solutions have to be found which 'overcome distributional obstacles by compensating the losers' – solutions which may, as likely as not, in the end defeat the initial objects.

Where decision-making is thus fraught with problems of efficiency anyway, and decision-making pathologies such as log-rolling and pork-barrel politics are common practice, it is hard to imagine that the proposed referenda could materially damage European politics. Even if one assumes that any additional veto-player will aggravate the problem (however slightly, according to the law of decreasing marginal costs), the question arises whether the direct-democratic character of the additional veto would not neutralise this effect. While the log may well roll among any kind of representatives, and roll on to any new actor included in the bargaining process, it is difficult to envisage the log rolling on to voters. On the contrary, one would expect a popular vote to induce representatives to step back from the package-deals just tied up, rather than an electorate being bribed into accepting a 'side-payment' so that they put up with some evil they abhor (like the loss of sterling or the Deutschmark, or the abolition of working hour regulations, or the inevitability of genetically-modified food).

Yet this does not wholly clear the proposal from the reproach of potentially harming the decision-making efficiency and system effectiveness. For two not altogether unlikely results of the electorate's not being 'so easily bribed' are (1) that a threatening veto is instrumentalised by the respective unit's representative(s) in a bargaining network (provided that they are in fact incorporated in it which, however, considering the networks' inherent lopsidedness, is not necessarily so) to increase side-payments; (2) that the direct-democratic veto indeed effectively breaks up the package-deal and thus puts an end to the process of problem solving in the case at hand. Since the compromise solution has then failed, there may be no solution at all to whatever problem there initially was. The latter seems the more probable outcome, in mid-term at any rate, possibly resulting in political immobility at the European level. In the longer run, however, a more electorally based log-rolling might reassert itself.

The Time Factor

With regard to the narrower notion of decision-making efficiency, the time factor has also to be taken into account. Empirical data show (see König & Schulz 1996) the time-lag between initial proposal and final decision to be remarkably short in European decision-making, considering its complexity and the frequent (if partly informal) requirement of unanimity. In the decade 1984 to 1994 the median time-lag was but 156 days; in only 14.5 per cent of cases it amounted to one year or more. Such unexpected speed can in part be explained by the comparatively great number of regulations and comparable decisions of a 'technical' kind which do not require a lengthy legislative process; with directives the time-lag was found to be considerably longer. Moreover, measures of agricultural and commercial policy, which account for more than two-thirds of the total number of proposals, required significantly less time than measures in any other issue areas. No doubt, this finding will have to be ascribed to the well-working and routinised issue networks in those two areas which have been at the core of European integration from the start, after all.

EC decision-making has, however, slowed down since the early 1990s. Although the introduction of qualified majority voting into Council procedures should have speeded up the process, this effect has been more than outdone by increased parliamentary participation. So here we have a striking example of the democracy-efficiency dilemma: both the participation of additional actors and the extension of democratic control obviously have the effect of slowing down decision-making, and inevitably so; for whenever widespread consensus about an issue is lacking (which will normally be the case), any proposal or initiative runs the risk of being blocked. What is true of parliamentary participation is also true, of course, of extended citizens' participation: the direct-democratic vetoes will have the same effect. In their case the effect of lengthening the process of arriving at a final decision may even be expected to be disproportionally great for the two reasons (1) that the referenda can only be started 'after the event', that is after the normal legislative process has come to its close; and (2) that the procedures first of petitioning and second of the referendum proper will take their time. The Swiss experience is an illustration for this point: including the referendum phase, major reform projects since the 1960s have taken up to twenty years to be implemented – or eventually to fail (Abromeit 1992b, p. 176f.). To be fair it must be mentioned, though, that there are other factors, apart from the referenda, which render Swiss federal decision-making exceptionally slow; even excluding the referendum phase, the time-lag between first proposal to final act is frequently one of several years. One should also bear in mind that decision-making in Europe will not generally be slowed down since the relevant referenda are not mandatory. Moreover, even if applied frequently, the optional referendum will be considerably less time-consuming than are, for instance, the procedures of judicial review (as practiced in Germany).

To sum up, it cannot be denied that the proposed direct-democratic instruments will reduce the efficiency of European decision-making in so far as they are apt to extend the time-lag between initial proposal and final decision, at times even considerably. Furthermore, one can reasonably assume that they will push up the costs of decision-making. The question of possible effects on system effectiveness cannot be answered quite so easily nor unequivocally. On the one hand, the instruments may have the beneficial effect of stemming the tide towards ever more costly package-deals. While they could thus be expected to pave the way for more adequate problem solving, they may on the other hand well be the means of preventing problem solving at all. Add to this the increased uncertainty about European law that will result from facilitating the revocation of European competences, and you will come to the conclusion that, on the whole, the vetoes will be detrimental to effectiveness, too. One further aspect, though, which may change the overall picture decisively ought not be disregarded. I mentioned above that European referenda would be likely to enhance a sense of European identity in those who participate. Being given the opportunity to contradict the decisions of 'them up there in Brussels' may at the same time gradually enhance the acceptance of European politics in general.

Biases And Asymmetries

There are more ambivalences that will have to be faced. As a means of paying due respect to different intensities of preferences, referenda are basically and inevitably asymmetric in so far as they privilege any group feeling very keenly about an issue, or any group *defending* particular rights (or their given status). Furthermore, since they are a means of enforcing the need for consensual decisions they tend to privilege the status quo. *Any* move towards unanimity can be said to do so, as any additional veto-player increases the risk of immobility. The question is (once again) whether the direct-democratic veto *adds* to these general risks and asymmetries and in a specific way, whether it generates biases of its own, and whether such effects are particularly detrimental in the European context.

A Middle-Class Bias

The first bias to be mentioned in this respect is that which results from the unequal propensity to vote: in modification of a well-known dictum (Schattschneider 1960), the choir of direct democracy sings with a pronounced middle-class accent (Linder 1994, p. 129). As I have already argued above, this bias will make itself felt the more in decision-making and distort policy results, the more the issues thus decided are those of common concern in which the whole populace ought to 'share an interest'. It will make itself less felt if the matter is one of concern to a specific unit or community, and in particular whenever entrenched rights are at stake. Since that is exactly the rationale of the direct-democratic veto we might be justified in discarding the participatory bias as irrelevant, were it not for the fact that in the case of the suggested sectoral veto it will frequently be impossible to distinguish the sectoral from the common concern. As I have repeatedly pointed out, one of the decisive advantages of the optional referendum is that it allows the inclusion of the 'second side' of the assumed sectoral unit, so often neglected in network (and group) politics. This 'second side', however, will in many cases simply be that of consumers and therefore be largely identical with the 'general public'.

So the middle-class bias has to be reckoned with, at least theoretically. Whether it will be a problem which leads to serious distortions in practice is, however, another matter. There is little reason to believe that a middle-class effect or higher education will significantly distort consumer interests,[9] and more reason to expect that identical 'shared risks' will be only more strongly felt in those quarters. Arguably the same applies to matters of environmental protection, to name another example of the 'second side' representing a basically common interest, the more so since in these borderline cases the awareness of 'shared risks' will frequently have a distinctly altruistic flavour and induce a more or less strong impetus to act vicariously. It must also be taken into account that the pervasive group and network politics are in their

---

9   They will do so in part, however, when the likely result of proposed measures of consumer protection is a price increase.

turn by no means symmetric and unbiased. They are primarily skewed towards producer interests, though, not least because these are most easily organised; in addition, the interests promoted by them are typically distorted by oligarchical structures and by the 'agents' becoming independent enough from their 'principals' to pursue objects of their own. If in fact the sectoral referenda should work in the expected manner, that is bring to bear the interests, costs or risks of the 'other side', then any specific bias constituted by uneven participation would merely be set off against this other bias, and hopefully attenuate the latter's detrimental effects.

In other words, the referenda will not introduce a bias and asymmetries to an otherwise non-selective policy-making system but add a different bias to an already biased one. Since there is no reason to suppose the biases to operate in the same direction matters will not be made worse but perhaps be improved because of counter-balancing effects. I confess that, in any case, I do not relish the criticism of the referenda's 'middle-class accent'. It does not seem justified to discard a participatory instrument – an opportunity at least to avert untoward policies – especially such an undemanding one like casting one's vote, for no other reason than that not all citizens grasp at it in the same eager way. On the contrary, I should trust that those whose preferences on the issues in question are sufficiently intense will not let themselves be detained; and that, if some do not use the instrument, it is not necessarily the instrument that is to blame.

Problems Of Inequality

All this reasoning applies to the sectoral veto. As for the regional veto, I have stated above that it is by necessity asymmetric because there are those regions which are of autonomous status and possess entrenched rights, and those who are (and do) not. This asymmetry cannot be helped and does not even need special justification. It is a fact that regions in Europe are of different status; and there is no reason whatever why those regions endowed with the right of self-government should lose it solely on the grounds that there are others which are not. Rather, whenever a community has been used to self-government, to infringe upon this status or even rob it of it, will have to be very carefully and thoroughly legitimised and hence require the consent of those who would suffer from the loss.

Another problem may be ticked off briefly, even though it is of some theoretical relevance. Any device nearing the voting rule of unanimity will prolong if not aggravate the underlying inequality of those who participate in decision-making. In discussing contract theory I have already alluded to the inequality dilemma: the more heterogeneous the society, the more consensual decision-making will have to be; yet the more consensual the latter is, the less will it be possible to reduce inequality (i.e., heterogeneity in socio-economic terms), for the better-off will block any move of a redistributive kind. This is why I suggested avoiding referenda on clearly redistributive issues, while acknowledging that this may be difficult to contrive in practice. Theoretically, there is no easy way out of this conundrum. But with regard to the practical problem at hand one only needs to point out that the processes of log-rolling and forming package-deals described above have just the same effect: moves which initially have been meant to diminish disparities are toned down in the complex European bargaining process to maintain the status quo of widely differing welfare levels. Whatever the other effects of the additional direct-democratic veto, it is unlikely (again) to make matters worse in this respect.

'Negative Integration'

There is no denying, however, that any additional veto must on the whole be considered an additional force to preserve the European status quo and presents a hindrance to more active (or interventionist) European governance. For obvious reasons such an effect is logically inevitable. If for any action to be taken collectively the consent of many actors is needed, action becomes difficult; it becomes next to impossible when unanimity is required, provided that actors' interests are sufficiently divergent. The obstacle may be overcome by side-payments (see above); or actors can agree to leave the respective decision(s) to some sort of single actor (a wise 'legislator' perhaps, or an independent agency, or simply state bureaucracy); or else they may agree not to undertake any collective action at all. Where no collective action (state intervention or regulation) had existed before, this latter 'default solution' implies that all of the single actors are left in peace to pursue their own interests individually (which is the solution libertarians like Buchanan would prefer anyway, see Buchanan 1990). If, on the other hand, the matter is one of improving regulations which are already in existence but have turned out to be unsatisfactory, the default solution prolongs this unhappy state of affairs. Both results have their obvious drawbacks

– in terms of external costs, injustice, and inefficiency – which need not be discussed in detail here. And both ways of preserving the status quo may easily be discovered in European politics, witness the long and fruitless efforts to achieve a common social policy or to reform the Common Agricultural Policy. Once more, the question is whether the introduction of direct-democratic instruments into European policy making would make matters significantly worse.

So far, European integration has had a definite 'negative' bias. With some few exceptions (the major one being agricultural policy) its main accent has been on 'liberalisation': first in the elimination of customs duties, then in the abolition of other barriers to the 'free flow of capital, goods and services' (though less of people) which used to exist in the shape of all manners of member-state regulations, be they of social policy, structural (and industrial) policy, monopoly prohibition, quality standards, consumer protection, environmental protection, or whatever. Liberalisation has, of course, been the main and explicit object of European integration from the start and is not to be laid at the door of unanimous decision-making. Yet as Scharpf (1996) argues, a distinct gap between 'negative' and 'positive integration' has opened up which may not have been initially intended. While 'positive integration', i.e., the agreement of 'common policies' likewise envisaged in the treaty, is 'subject to all of the impediments facing European intergovernmental policy making', 'negative integration' has been impelled 'without much political intention, through interventions of the European Commission against infringements of Treaty obligations, and through the decisions and preliminary rulings of the European Court of Justice' (ibid., p. 15).[10] This basic asymmetry results in its turn in a 'competency gap, in which national policy is severely restrained in its problem-solving capacity, while European policy is constrained by the lack of intergovernmental agreement.' (ibid.). One may as well add that the asymmetry between negative and positive integration corresponds in practice with the asymmetry between the protection of capital and the support of labour interests (Streeck 1995): 'decision by non-

10 The difference, which according to Scharpf is 'a fundamental institutional' one, is however basically a consequence of the character of legal norms: 'libertarian' rights fending off state interference do not normally require collective action (and such are the stipulations in the treaty concerning the 'free flow'); whereas 'social rights' (granting favours, guaranteeing welfare levels, etc.) do. Hence the former are immediately applicable (and enforceable by Courts), and the latter merely 'programmatic'.

decision' at the transnational level invariably benefits employers and in the shape of liberalisation strengthens them at the national level as well, whereas any move to meet the demands of labour requires positive action at both levels.

So the matter is not merely one of privileging the status quo. Instead, there are two biases to be dealt with: one is towards inertia and non-decision in general, which does indeed favour the European status quo – that is, the status quo of integration. The other, however, while on the face of it closely related to the first in that it likewise seems to stem from non-decision-making, is not exactly towards the status quo but rather towards a kind of status quo ante, regarding social, redistributive etc., standards reached at member-state level. Negative integration in fact alters the status quo in some of the member states by implying a certain roll-back of social and other achievements.

It is important to distinguish these two biases when it comes to judging the effects of direct-democratic vetoes on European decision-making. It is, moreover, important to realise that liberalisation and negative integration do not only occur by way of (political, legislative) non-decision but are also enforced by manifest legislative action. The answer to our question is then a twofold one: in so far as the referenda introduce an additional veto-player into an already complex and super-majoritarian decision-making system they will inevitably make matters worse, i.e., give further strength to those forces which tend to favour the European status quo, put a brake on European governance and slow down the pace of further integration. Yet this effect must not be mistaken for a bias in favour of the overall societal status quo, or even status quo ante, nor for the passive state. Instead, the referenda may in some cases also turn out to put a brake on further negative integration: when they are directed against a directive forcing member states to relinquish one or other of their national policies, or when they veto (or even revoke) a certain policy to be settled at the European level. Hence, while formally privileging the status quo and the 'inactive (super-)state', they may have quite the opposite effect as regards content.

Depending on points of view, interests and objects, as well as on the policy areas and on the types of decisions primarily considered, this effect will be judged to be either detrimental or beneficial for overall system performance. There are certainly cases in which the European status quo thus sheltered tends to take the shape of a 'race-down' (witness the dangers of social dumping, and the threat of irreversible destruction of the environment) and where collective action at the European level,[11] or even decisions by a 'super-enforcing agency', would seem to be most urgently needed to prevent the worst coming to the worst. But as it seems, such moves are by their nature more likely to be blocked in the Council than by the veto of (say) consumers acting on the spur of the growing risks they fear to share.

The *acquis communautaire*

In sum, the predictable effects of the proposed direct-democratic vetoes are by no means unequivocal. As regards decision-making efficiency, the likely advantage of breaking up costly package-deals and hindering side-payments will be counterbalanced by a tendency to slow down the decision-making process or even to prevent decisions being taken, or becoming effective, at all. Whether or not the overall system effectiveness will on balance be positively or negatively influenced must remain an open question. One should bear in mind, though, that the negative trait of cumbersome decision-making is already inherent in European politics at present, and is unlikely to be materially worsened. Moreover, any judgement on the net consequences of system effectiveness will have to take into account elusive factors such as the increasing acceptance of European politics or a growing sense of European identity, induced by referenda.

Expectations are equally ambiguous as regards the probable biases introduced, enhanced or toned down by direct-democratic means. An increase in the number of veto groups will in general not only reduce the speed of decision-making processes and the number of collective decisions taken, but will in particular block any decisions of a redistributive nature and hence privilege the status quo. Again, this is a feature of European decision-making as it already works at present. If the additional veto does aggravate this weakness, it is doubtful whether it will do so materially. On the other side of the balance, there is the direct-democratic element

---

11 However, especially with regard to environmental protection European policies appear so far to have led to a certain roll-back of standards of the more advanced communities. Observers fear that the Amsterdam agreement will even enforce this trend of 'negative integration' on the pretext of protecting the 'functioning of the internal market' (see the new paragraphs 3 to 9 to replace par. 3 to 5 of Art. 100a TEC).

which may put the brakes on further liberalisation, or negative integration, since the legislative acts to be vetoed at the European level are (not least because of the national governments alternately blocking any more active common policies in the Council) more likely to be acts abolishing regulations and interventions than acts introducing them. This latter possible effect indicates that it is virtually impossible to arrive at an overall judgement on the way direct democracy works, for this way depends decisively on the nature of the surrounding political system. The effects to be expected from the introduction of optional referenda into a heretofore smooth-running national decision-making set will probably differ entirely from the effects they may have within the supranational, non-statist, highly complex policy-making arrangements in the EU.

With the introduction of the direct-democratic vetoes, however, especially if combined with the opportunity to revoke community competences, the European *acquis communautaire* must certainly be less safe than it used to be. Until now, all European actors have agreed on the common objective never to fall back behind the standard once reached in integration, harmonisation, and in the institutionalisation of the European polity. In particular, the 'non-intergovernmental' institutions created – the Commission, the EP and the ECJ – soon proved to be valiant safeguards of this *acquis*, and moreover eager promoters of its expansion. Yet the *acquis communautaire* is a strange and elusive being: it is rather uneven (because of opt-outs and the separate moves of a 'core Europe'); it is one of uncertain dimensions (because it rests to a considerable extent on the ECJ's reading of EU primary law, and on the momentum with which it endows the treaty's inherent teleology[12]); and above all it is not identical with what had been agreed in the initial contract(s).

The mutual obligation 'to maintain in full the *acquis communautaire* and build on it' was explicitly laid down in the Maastricht Treaty (Art. B), although the parties to the contract appear to have agreed to their pledge tongue in cheek for apart from managing partly to step back from it in the Protocols annexed to this document (see Curtin 1993, p. 44ff.), they at the same time provided for a general re-examination of the treaty's provisions in the 1996(f.)

---

12 Arguably, leaving the task of developing constitutional law to constitutional judges amounts to accepting a considerable degree of legal uncertainty, for the judges' interpretation of constitutional norms will invariably differ from the written text, and vary over time. After a while it will grow difficult if not impossible to know beforehand whether one is digressing from these norms or not.

Intergovernmental Conference (Art. N). Hence the uncertainty surrounding the *acquis* extends to its quality of being legally binding, too. European lawyers from different quarters do not obviously see eye-to-eye on the questions both of its binding force and of its gradual extension; British lawyers, for instance, most emphatically disagree with those of the European Courts on the Social Charter's forming a part of the acquis and on its binding the British government.[13]

But even if the contractual situation were more clear-cut, it is debatable whether it is wise to insist upon the *acquis communautaire's* being sacrosanct. The EU is not a state, not even a federation, and the legal basis of its policies is not a constitution but a contract. Any other contract is open to any sort of revision once unanimity amongst its parties about the appropriateness and validity of its norms is lost. As things stand in Europe, it is unlikely for such an event to happen concerning basic principles. Yet resentment with the very core of integration may well grow if loss of unanimity about its details is sanctioned instead of being allowed in due course to lead to a revision. To provide for a general reversibility is all the more advisable since much of what has come to be regarded as part of the *acquis communautaire* has never been properly consented to by all parties to the contract but happened to be included in a rather opaque way. Moreover, much of what has thus developed has proved meanwhile to be detrimental to one or other of the member countries' interests, incompatible with their basic political cultures or simply ineffectual. I am not arguing here the point that revisions and revocations should occur whenever one of the national governments, for reasons of their own (which will often be electoral ones), sees fit to do so; but I am much inclined to advocate a revisionary process to set in whenever the people do wish so. Contrary to most federations, the treaty envisages a kind of minor 'right of secession' in the shape of the opt-out. It does, however, reject the opportunity to alter the allocation of powers once agreed upon in both directions,[14] usually envisaged by federalist constitutions. There is little plausibility in a

13 Witness the controversy on the ECJ ruling of 12 November 1996, which forces the British government to apply a 1993 EU directive on working hours in the U.K. The ECJ ruled thus because the directive was not formally based on the Social Charter. At the bottom of the conflict, however, is the uncertainty about whether or not the Protocols annexed to the TEU are in fact to be regarded as 'integral parts' of the Treaty, Art. 239 TEC notwithstanding.

14 See Art. N(2) TEU which allows for the re-examination of the provisions of the Treaty but not for all of them, and attempts to bind the revision to the unalterable *acquis communautaire* of Art. B.

supranational entity's sticking to an *acquis communautaire* more rigidly than federal states do, and to grant to its units' peoples less right to have it their own way.

The Evasion Of Politics

One of the reasons, of course, why the *acquis* acquired its present prominent position is the weakness of European politics, and the 'weak basic political consensus among the political powers' (Curtin 1993, p. 62) in particular. Apparently those political powers themselves felt that their fragile consensus ought not to be threatened by the existence of a permanent option of breaking away. So they kind of formally retreated even from their alleged role of 'masters of the treaty' to hide behind the *acquis communautaire* and the back of the judges, thereby mutually convincing each other that there was no escape from the one-way dynamic of integration and of strengthening the Union.

The intricacies of consensus politics must not, however, by necessity lead to the retreat of politics nor to the handing over to the courts.[15] There are alternative ways of dealing with them, not least the one to 'bring the people in' (see Hedetoft 1994, p. 143). But while there may be a good case for leaving the final decision on crucial questions to the people, there is no denying that direct-democratic instruments may well trigger off a similar dynamic. For in order to avoid their application, political actors will evince an even more pressing need for consensus politics. This in its turn will strengthen if not double the European politicians' urge to minimise 'political action' and the amount of 'responsible' decision-making, and instead to hide behind independent agencies.

Tendencies such as these undoubtedly exist (see Majone 1994), regardless of elements of direct democracy being practised. They are little likely to be remedied by them, because whatever else the latter's advantages may be, they will certainly not make European politics less complicated. So with or without them, the European *acquis communautaire* is on a fair way of growing ever more uncertain. In the guise of being maintained by disinterested experts it may in the end be lost in a haze of irresponsibilities.

---

15 Dicey (1959, p. 157ff.) for one firmly believed this to be the inevitable consequence even of federalism, and many observers have done so since.

7

MODELS AND REALITIES

Advantages And Drawbacks: On Balance

Direct-democratic vetoes may well be the only means of providing for a modicum of democratic accountability in the case of politics as complex, as multi-dimensional, as much 'variable in geometry' and as much interspersed with decision-making by independent, quasi-non-political agencies, as European politics are. Parliamentarianism, at any rate, whether bi- or multicameral, does not in the least allow for a similar degree of flexibility, neither at the national nor at the supranational level. A further parliamentarisation of European politics is, moreover, apt to promote further centralisation and must therefore be expected to aggravate the EU's incompatibility problems as well as its internal conflicts. In contrast, the proposed direct-democratic devices permit the different political systems of the combined 'old nations' to coexist with the new European one in a way resembling a unit construction system: where units remain intact while cooperating and joining a separate common policy-making super-structure and where at the same time boundaries between the levels are sufficiently permeable to facilitate direct control by people at all levels. Enlarging upon this analogy, one may add that the proposed device also makes it possible to fit together different types of units. It allows the complementing of the traditional territorial type of unit with a 'new' sectoral one, thus answering the need to find remedies for the growing loss of congruence in democratic politics.

There is another material advantage which must not be overlooked: European parliamentarianism, if left to itself, will for a long time to come suffer from the lack of infrastructure in the shape of European parties, associations and public opinion; it will in a way be a representative body lacking representees. In such a situation, the referenda can be assumed to act as a kind of substitute first, but then – in rousing Europe's various peoples over European issues – as a means of gradually developing just that infrastructure. They may make up for the deficit commonly identified as one of the major obstacles in the path of the EU's further democratisation, simply by way of providing opportunities for direct participation.

This picture of manifold advantages is, of course, incomplete without reference to the drawbacks enumerated in the last chapter. Yet there is a decisive difference between the two worth dwelling upon. The gains it is to be hoped will be achieved by the direct-democratic device are not to be obtained by any other means, whereas the drawbacks are those of possibly aggravating weaknesses and inefficiencies *already* inherent in the European policy-making system. They result mainly from the latter's complexity and from the number of veto-players, which is great at present and cannot be significantly reduced in a society as heterogeneous and as loosely connected as the European one without causing even more drawbacks, and more serious ones. Instead of an 'ever closer Union', the EU after Maastricht has been dubbed an 'ever more complicated Union' (*The Economist* 30 March 1996, p. 25), and the proposed vetoes would undoubtedly add to this tendency. They will particularly add to the obstacles in the path of active governance in Europe. Yet at the same time they may in part make up for this deficit by blocking negative integration as well, leaving it to member states to pursue their more active interventionist policies.

On balance, I would judge the gains in democratic legitimacy to outweigh the losses in decision-making efficiency, with the overall effect on system effectiveness hovering somewhat uncertainly in the middle: acceptance will probably grow, but European harmonisation as well as regulating activities will lose momentum. Yet if there is any truth in the belief widely held in Western democracies that governance has to rely the more on the consent of citizens the more active it is, then the effect of slowing down the pace of European politics cannot wholly be judged to be a drawback. Instead, a certain inertia must then be accepted as an unavoidable trait of governance in a society where consent is difficult to achieve. In a non-state super-structure overarching a heterogeneous conglomerate of societies governance can only proceed at a slow pace if it is to be legitimate. It is, in the longer term at any rate, a risky course to push forward with active governance without at the same time providing ways for meaningful citizen participation: of creating opportunities to withhold consent effectively.

Who Supports Direct Democracy?

Whatever the net advantages of direct-democratic veto rights added to the existing institutions of European decision-making may be, the question remains whether there are any actors on the European stage who are at all likely to adopt the idea and set forth with attempts at its implementation. Here indeed the picture looks bleak. At best, I should imagine, one would find those who are 'not much opposed' to the project, once small groups of idealistic would-be reformers who are not heeded by politicians anyway are discarded. The group 'Eurotopia', for instance, in 1995 launched the proposal of a popular initiative to set in motion a process of constitution building proper, which was supposed to be followed up by a referendum on the final document drawn up by a European constituent assembly. None of the European institutions nor any of the member-state governments warmed to the idea, not even the EP, although its Institutional Committee is strongly in favour of a European constitution and submitted an own draft version in 1994.[1] Nor could, apparently, the support of the Austrian and Italian governments be secured. Both are somewhat experienced with direct-democratic instruments and themselves suggested in 1996 a popular petition as a means for citizens at least to influence the European agenda. The Council's Reflection Group and the Commission's Task Force for the IGC incidentally seem to have discussed the introduction of direct-democratic elements into European decision-making but dismissed it; as you are told in Brussels 'the idea was there but has been lost meanwhile'.

Judging by their presumed interests, neither of the European institutions can at first sight be expected to favour the idea of direct-democratic vetoes. The Commission will strongly object to any device which threatens to be detrimental to active European governance. The EP will do so for the same reason, nor will MEPs at all relish their acts being set aside by direct interference of their voters. Council members will, in addition, have good cause to dread being positively disavowed by their 'own' peoples, a feat which would mar their

1   See Second Report of the Institutional Committee on the Constitution of the European Union (Herman Report) of 9 February 1994.

negotiative powers in Europe considerably. Yet that such an effect of the new vetoes might not be at all unlikely, may somewhat allay the Commission's misgivings: regional and sectoral vetoes might at closer inspection be more palatable to them than those exercised by national governments, not least because the former will probably be less frequent and at any rate less strategically induced.

Predictably, the reactions of member states will similarly oscillate between caution, misgiving, and downright rejection. They will, however, not always be in line with the respective political traditions. British governments, for instance, could possibly detect some charm in a device that can be expected to put an additional brake on further centralisation in Europe, their general distrust of any kind of direct democracy notwithstanding. The German and the French governments (of whatever political colour) will foreseeably be most strongly opposed to any instrument apt to confirm a suspicion that European integration has all along been promoted by a political class increasingly alienated from their peoples. In fact the only country's political class that could be expected to support the project is that of Switzerland which is no member yet not least because of the Union's lack of permeability, with regard to the participatory rights of people on the peripheries. But even Swiss political élites increasingly debate the pros and cons of direct democracy nowadays, in part apparently sorely tempted to abandon core constitutional principles for fear of being isolated and of mutating into an 'alpine zoo'.[2]

One should add that governments will generally be little inclined to take kindly to direct-democratic devices. Their 'natural' interest is to minimise democratic control of their actions, to minimise the probability of being voted out of office and thus to maximise their own political autonomy in their home countries. There are observers who judge exactly this urge to be one of the main motives for pushing ahead with European integration: governments trade the losses in 'state autonomy' incurred in intergovernmental cooperation against gains in 'internal autonomy' and instrumentalise the EU as a shield against domestic participatory pressures (see Wolf 1998). In that view, the EU's democratic deficit is not a chance byproduct of integration, but was firmly intended by major actors from the start. Hence, where the EU's democratisation is concerned, not much hope should be placed in these actors.

2 A conference on the question of 'how much direct democracy Switzerland can bear with' in future, held in July 1997, may serve as an example; see Borner & Rentsch 1997.

The European Agenda And The Amsterdam Summit

In European reality the debate on democratic deficits has meanwhile subsided to a surprising degree anyway. Other topics have dominated the agenda, mainly the EMU and the Euro: when EMU is really to start; whether it had not better be postponed; who is to join and who to decide on this question;[3] whether or not the criteria for joining ought be softened. On the face of it this is an economic debate; yet at the bottom of it is the major political (albeit in some countries firmly tabooed) question whether anyone wants to have the Euro at all. Polls at least show that scepticism and distrust are widespread, nearly everywhere.[4] Consequently, governments increasingly get into stormy waters at home and meet with growing resistance to the austerity policies somewhat desperately endorsed with the object of meeting the 'Maastricht criteria'.

The other major topic on the agenda of the 1996(f.) IGC (or 'Maastricht II') which was brought to its close in Amsterdam in June 1997 was the decision-making rules in the Council, or more precisely: the extended application of qualified majority voting. It is judged by most European politicians to be a necessary precondition of the enlargement of the EU: without QMV, but with a growing number of members, all progress in integration will, or so it is feared, come to its end; with QMV, however, we have been told that no choice between either widening or deepening the Union will have to be made, for the one would no longer exclude the other. Yet not all of the member states agree with this reasoning. On the contrary, debate on this subject has been as prolonged as it has been heated – not only because of the British government's most strongly vetoing the loss of its veto. The change of government in the U.K. may have changed the tone but not the tenor of the debate. So in the end, QMV was extended to some minor issues but the veto kept up in all major policy areas.

Since this outcome was predictable, a new magic formula was invented and put on the IGC agenda at the Dublin summit of December 1996, by a combined French-German effort: a 'flexibility

3 When the Swedish government declared in June 1997 that it did not intend to join the EMU immediately, the European public learnt to its amazement that the President of the Commission meant to stick to the letter to the Maastricht Treaty according to which it is for the Council to decide upon which of the 'qualified' member states are to join the EMU's first stage.

4 National polls do, at any rate. The Eurobarometer does still assert that an average of 48 per cent of European citizens is in favour of the Euro. See Eurobarometer 44/96, p. 56.

clause' to be entered into the treaty is meant to facilitate, even to encourage closer integration of only a part of the member states, with the others progressing more slowly, or remaining at the present level, or even opting out of common policies. A modicum of such flexibility of course exists already. The clause adopted on the Amsterdam summit now puts it on a firm legal basis, lays down procedures and allows for its more systematic application. The formula (which is a mere renaming of the 'Europe of different speeds' anyway) may, however, prove as dishonest as it may endanger the Union in its present composition: dishonest because it has already happened that members who had not consented to certain integrative steps were afterwards nonetheless forced by the Courts to comply with them (or by their bankers, or by foreign investors, for that matter); and endangering because the gaps between members moving with different speeds will inevitably widen in the course of time and may well lead to unforeseen and unintended break-ups in the end. In a much-ridiculed metaphor various European politicians (mainly French and German ones) have likened the Union to a convoy and have lamented that the slowest ship should not determine the speed of whole convoy – not realising that there is no convoy if it does not.

Other topics had been on the agenda of the IGC to revise the Maastricht Treaty: other aspects of institutional reform (concerning the EP and the Commission); an incorporation of the 'second and third pillar' of the EU into the institutional and procedural framework of the EC and especially the incorporation of the Schengen agreements into the framework of 'common policies'; improvements for the 'European citizens' including their social rights. At the last minute (and as a consequence of the change of the French government) an additional 'employment chapter' was to be considered. Most of the treaty revisions actually agreed upon are rather marginal. The biggest changes occured in the 'third pillar' of justice and home affairs, concerning immigration and asylum policies as well as cooperation in the combat of crime via 'Europol'. The 'Schengen *acquis*' will henceforth be part of the TEU although the UK and Ireland opted out and Denmark insists upon special treatment.[5] Council decisions in this area will, however, require unanimity. Europol will be considerably extended but will

5 Austria however, eager to be a party to the 'Schengen Club', achieved its object of being fully accepted only after prolonged struggles, although the revised treaty supported its claim. Opposition came mainly from the Germans whose government was in its turn put under pressure by Bavarians.

remain firmly located in the sphere of intergovernmental cooperation. Both areas of Justice and Home Affairs will, incidentally, be removed from parliamentary control: at the European level the EP will only be 'informed' (at best), and at the national level governments will be shielded by the supranational agreements. Concerning the Common Foreign and Security Policy things remain basically unchanged. The new chapter on employment is exceedingly vague and does not really constitute a new responsibility of the community, apart from the 'promotion of coordination' of member states' employment policies.

Surprisingly enough, an extensive chapter on the principle of subsidiarity has been added to the treaty. Although consisting of thirteen paragraphs it does not alter the ambivalence of the principle as stated in Art. 3 b TEC, nor the bias towards community competences. It does, however, envisage the possibility of community action 'to be ... discontinued, where it is no longer justified' (ch. 9 par. 3 Amsterdam Treaty). It does not require the community to pay respect to any regional competences but at least to take account of financial (or other) burdens falling on local authorities, as a consequence of community action (par. 9). It will be a matter of further debate to decide whether these extensive explanations of the principle will be of political relevance or merely of symbolic value. The same is true for the alterations concerning the EP. Its powers of co-decision are increased, the procedures slightly simplified; but the EP will remain to be a 'second-class' legislator, lacking full budget control and equal status with the Council.

Matters of institutional reform aimed at remedying the democratic deficit and of extended citizen participation put on the agenda immediately after Maastricht I have got lost in the course of subsequent summits. The recommendations of the Council's Reflection Group and of the Commission's Task Force[6] had been rather modest anyway and amounted to hardly more than a clarification and simplification of procedures and of EU primary law: the latter was to be rewritten in order to make European citizens unterstand at last what the EU was about. In the Amsterdam Treaty this is mirrored by the demand (in chapter 11) to improve the drafting of Community legislation, in order to be 'better understood by the public and in business circles'. Apart from that, the move to render the Union more democratic and to

6 See also the draft version for a revision of the treaties, submitted to the Dublin summit in December 1996.

enhance its appeal to citizens has come down to the 'Citizens First' campaign, launched by the EP and the Commission on 26 November 1996, a campaign which is essentially one of advertising and, secondly, one of providing information.[7] Apparently it has not been able to cause a great stir among the various peoples since.

The Decrease Of Support

In the absence of institutional reform of either the simplifying or the democratising kind, the EU will be left with all its problems of decision-making inefficiency, system ineffectiveness and political biases, and with a legitimatory gap which will widen further – the more so, perhaps, the more the inefficiencies induce a sort of 'out-sourcing' of politics into independent agencies, the dealings of which are yet more opaque to citizens and the general public than those of the normal institutional set of European decision-making. The citizens react with a withdrawal of support. Recently (since 1989, to be precise) Eurobarometer polls have shown new lowest scores in overall support for the EU and for European integration every year.[8] Fewer than half of the EU's population now support the principle as such, or think that EU membership is advantageous for their countries, although supporters of the EU still outnumber those who would rather secede. Support is, incidentally, lowest in the countries which have recently joined (Sweden, Finland, and Austria). Identification with Europe and 'feeling as a European citizen' has never been a strong point in people's support for Europe (which is one of the reasons for talking about a 'permissive consensus': depicting support as the mere toleration of integration instead of the forming of a positive allegiance).[9] It seemed to grow gradually in the early 1980s but weakened in the 1990s. In this as in other areas the nation-state, and feelings of national identity, have reasserted themselves in the meantime.

The Eurobarometer polls should not be over-interpreted. They have at any rate to be qualified by the exceedingly high degree of ignorance on European matters. Alterations in support cannot be assumed to be based on knowledge allowing sophisticated

---

7 Every European citizen may, for instance, ring certain telephone numbers in their respective country, free of charge, to gain information about European facilities, etc. This is, apparently, the institutions' notion of the citizens' exercising their 'right to know and be heard' (which is the campaign's motto).

8 For the following see Eurobarometer 44/96; *Guardian Weekly*, 5 January 1997.

9 See for this Hedetoft (1994, p. 22) who talks of 'negative identification'.

evaluation but will to a considerable degree mirror common prejudices as well as more general feelings of content or discontent which may or may not be caused by the failures and achievements of European policies; at best, people will have a rather hazy notion of the latter. The somewhat surprisingly high percentages of citizens favouring the full parliamentarisation of the Union must be seen in the same light. Answers to the respective questions reflect support for the notion that any government should be made responsible to a parliament, rather than the concrete wish to see the EP strengthened. Once questions become more detailed, it soon becomes obvious that the European electorate is ill informed about the role the EP actually plays in European politics (and, interestingly enough, tends to overrate it[10]), and does not think twice about the likely consequences of its upgrading. Moreover, the expressed opinions on the EU's parliamentarisation bear little relation to overt behaviour: witness the low and decreasing turnout in European elections. The European citizens (who are as such still largely non-existent) are, however, not to be reproached for their ignorance and lack of interest. European politics are in fact wholly remote from them, and the way the EP operates and is elected does not contribute to reducing this distance. Elections are fought on national, not European issues. The latter are barely discussed, sometimes even tabooed (as is in Germany, for instance, the question of the desirability of an early monetary union[11]); information on them is scanty. So if European voters are expected to form their own opinions on European politics, what are they to base them on?

Lack of interest, information and identification in European citizens are, in common with the low turnout, both an indication of lacking democratic legitimacy and a cause of the prolongation and even widening of the EU's legitimatory gap, which in its turn originates from the lack of proper democratic accountability. The sort of legitimacy which derives from accountability, control and participation still rests rather exclusively with nation-states. The latter, however, suffer increasingly from a 'competency gap' (Scharpf 1996), following from the decreasing ability to solve problems within the confines of the national units. Both deficits

10 See the respective figures in Eurobarometer 44/96, p. 67.
11 It has become a habit among leading German politicians (with some few exceptions), instead of providing arguments in favour of EMU, to stress the necessity of European integration for the preservation of peace – which is obviously a trifle off the point.

constitute the dilemma of lacking 'congruence', frequently alluded to in the course of this book. According to quite a number of authors, there is one way out of this dilemma, and an apparently simple one at that. It is to place trust in the superior problem-solving capacity of the greater unit, which will in due course make up for any legitimatory gaps in proving to be a source of legitimacy in itself (Jachtenfuchs 1995, p. 129).

Yet there is at present little hope that such 'legitimisation by performance' will work. Eurobarometer findings show that citizens do indeed expect the community to perform in a superior way in a number of policy areas,[12] ranging from matters of foreign policy to environmental protection, consumer protection, employment, or even agricultural policy (which ought to remind us of the qualifications made above, with respect to survey results). Their expectations are, however, increasingly disappointed. Irrespective of any decision-making problems, European policies have in many areas resulted in interest politics of the worst possible kind and must in the eyes of the beholder appear to cause irrationalities of an alarming degree. No citizen fully in possession of his senses will ever be able to understand why goods (including live stock) have to be carried criss-cross for thousands of miles all over Europe before they are allowed to reach their destinations; he fails to see why European institutions take member countries severely to task over any attempts to ban imports of possibly infected or contaminated food and at the same time prove unwilling to take those to task who may be responsible for the contamination;[13] he has little forbearance with the community's obvious failure to come to grips with the alarming amount of fraud that has sprung up in the wake of European regulations, to name but a few instances. In the run-up to EMU things have got even worse. The austerity policies enacted by many of the member states in order to be one of the party in 1999 cannot but arouse suspicions that European integration is nothing but a means of rendering the rich richer, and the poor poorer; of increasing unemployment, weakening the unions, and of putting an end to the 'welfare state'; and of leading the European countries back, in many respects, into the nineteenth century.

12 See Eurobarometer 44/96, p. 70. Schmitt & Scheuer (1996), building on the findings of the European electoral study of 1994, come to similar results.
13 The BSE crisis, for instance, would have been half as bitter and dramatic if the Commission had adopted a firm stance at its beginning instead of attempting to hush up the affair in the interest of producers and to ignore potential dangers. In this particular case the EP has not proved to be an effective instrument of control, either.

To cut a long argument short: a modicum both of participation and of system effectiveness (and resulting acceptance) are needed to legitimise governance that claims to meet the standards of democratic government. So far the EU fails in both respects. Unfortunately, the economic situation is such that remedies cannot any longer be sought at nation-state level. Even apart from economic interconnections, many policy problems are either fraught with spill-overs and interdependencies, or of a sectoral nature cross-cutting national boundaries. This lands us with a bleak prospect: should democratic governance be impossible in future, after all, both at the nation-state and at the supranational level? Little chance of effective governance seems to be left for nation-states and little chance of democracy for supranational governance. Yet as for the latter, the main thing lacking may perhaps be an inventive mood. Something, at any rate, will have to be done.

BIBLIOGRAPHY

Abromeit, H. 'Korrektive parlamentarischer Mehrheitsherrschaft: Ein Überblick', *Zeitschrift für Parlamentsfragen*, vol. 18, no. 3, 1987, pp. 420–35
—— *Der verkappte Einheitsstaat*. Opladen, 1992a
—— 'Kontinuität oder "Jekyll-and-Hyde-Politik"', in *Staatstätigkeit in der Schweiz*, eds. H. Abromeit and W. Pommerehne, Bern, 1992b, pp.159–192
—— 'Föderalismus: Modelle für Europa', *Österreichische Zeitschrift für Politikwissenschaft*, vol. 22, no. 2, 1993, pp. 207–20
—— 'Volkssouveränität, Parlamentssouveränität, Verfassungssouveränität: Drei Realmodelle der Legitimation staatlichen Handelns', *Politische Vierteljahresschrift*, vol. 36, no. 1, 1995, pp. 49–66
Abromeit, H. and Pommerehne, W., eds., *Staatstätigkeit in der Schweiz*. Bern, 1992
Andersen, S.S. and Eliassen, K.A., eds., *The European Union: How Democratic is it?* London, 1996
Ballestrem, K.G. 'Die Idee des impliziten Gesellschaftsvertrages', in *Gerechtigkeit, Diskurs oder Macht?*, eds. L. Kern and H.P. Müller. Opladen, 1986, pp. 35–44
Barker, R. *Political Ideas in Modern Britain*. London, 1978
Beck, U. *Die Erfindung des Politischen*. Frankfurt/Main, 1993
Bentley, A.F. *The Process of Government*. Chicago, 1908
Benz, A. 'Regionalpolitik zwischen Netzwerkbildung und Institutionalisierung', *Staatswissenschaften und Staatspraxis*, vol. 7, no. 1, 1996, pp. 23–42
Benz, A., Scharpf, F.W. and Zintl, R. *Horizontale Politikverflechtung. Zur Theorie von Verhandlungssystemen*. Frankfurt/Main and New York, 1992
Berger, P.A. *Individualisierung. Statusunsicherheit und Erfahrungsvielfalt*. Opladen, 1996
Blöchliger, H. and Frey, R. 'Der schweizerische Föderalismus: Ein Modell für den institutionellen Aufbau der Europäischen Union?', *Außenwirtschaft*, no. 4, 1992, pp. 515–48
Bodin, J. *Les Six Livres de la République*. 1583
Bohley, P. 'Über die Voraussetzungen von Föderalismus und die Bedeutung kollektiver Identität', in *Steuerrecht – Verfassungsrecht – Finanzpolitik*, eds. P. Kirchhof, K. Offerhaus and H. Schöberle. Köln, 1994, pp. 541–59
Bohnet, J. and Frey, B.S. 'Direct-Democratic Rules for a Future Europe – the Role of Discussion', *KYKLOS*, vol. 47, no. 3, 1994, pp. 341–54
Borner, S. and Rentsch, M. eds. *Wieviel direkte Demokratie verträgt die Schweiz?* Chur, 1997
Brennan, J. and Buchanan, J. *The Reason of Rules. Constitutional Political Economy*. Cambridge, 1985

Breton, A. and Scott, A. *The Economic Constitution of Federal States*. Toronto, 1978

Brittan, L. *Europe. The Europe we Need*. London, 1994

Buchanan, J.M. *The Limits of Liberty. Between Anarchy and Leviathan*. Chicago and London, 1975

—— 'Europe's Constitutional Opportunity', in *Europe's Constitutional Future*, ed. Institute of Economic Affairs. London, 1990, pp. 1–20

Buchanan, J.M. and Tullock, G. *The Calculus of Consent. Logical Foundations of Constitutional Democracy*. Ann Arbor, 1965 (1962)

Budge, I. *The New Challenge of Direct Democracy*. Cambridge, 1996

Budge, I., Crewe, I. and Farlie, D., eds. *Party Identification and Beyond*. London, 1976

Butler, D. and Ranney, A., eds. *Referendums around the World: The Growing Use of Direct Democracy*. Washington DC, 1994

BverfGE 89, 155. *Maastricht-Verdict*. 1993

Campbell, A., Converse, P.E., Miller, W.E. and Stokes, D.E. *Elections and the Political Order*. New York, London and Sydney, 1966

Christiansen, T. 'Gemeinsinn und europäische Integration. Strategien zur Optimierung von Demokratie- und Integrationsziel', in *Demokratie in Europa: Zur Rolle der Parlamente. (Zeitschrift für Parlamentsfragen*, special issue), eds. W. Steffani and U. Thaysen. Opladen, 1995, pp. 50–64

Cohen, J. and Rogers, J. 'Secondary Associations and Democratic Governance', *Politics & Society* 20 (no. 4 – special issue), 1992, pp. 393–472

—— 'Solidarity, Democracy, Association', in *Staat und Verbände. (Politische Vierteljahresschrift*, special issue, no. 25), ed. W. Streeck. Opladen, 1994, pp. 136–59

Cole, G.D.H. 'A Memorandum on the Question: What legislation is best designed to reduce antagonisms, to conciliate the interest of employers and employees, to coordinate the special activities of all enterprises and to harmonize the interests of producers and consumers?', in *Etude du Statut de la Production et du Role du Capital*, eds. G.D.H. Cole, T.N. Carver and C. Brinkmann. Brussels, 1938, pp. 1–60

—— *Social Theory*. London, 1970 (1920)

Conlan, T. 'Politics and Governance: Conflicting Trends in the 1990s', *The Annals of the American Academy of Political and Social Science*, vol. 509, 1990, pp. 128–38

Curtin, D. 'The Institutional Structure of the Union: A Europe of Bits and Pieces', *Common Market Law Review*, no. 30, 1993, pp. 17–69

Dahl, R.A. 'Federalism and the Democratic Process', in *Liberal Democracy*, eds. R. Pennock and J.W. Chapman, New York, 1983, pp. 95–108

—— *Democracy and its Critics*. New Haven, 1989

—— 'A Democratic Dilemma: System Effectiveness versus Citizen Participation', *Political Science Quarterly*, vol. 109, no. 1, 1994, pp. 23–34

Dahrendorf, R. 'Elemente einer Theorie des sozialen Konflikts', in *Gesellschaft und Freiheit*, ed. R. Dahrendorf. München, 1962, pp. 197–235

Dehousse, R. 'Constitutional Reform in the European Community: Are there "Alternatives to the Majoritarian Avenue"?', *West European Politics*, vol. 18, no. 3, 1995, pp. 118–31

Dehousse, R. and Christiansen, T., eds. *What Model for the Committee of the Regions? Past Experiences and Future Perspectives*, EUI Working Paper EUF no. 95/2. Florence, 1995

Deuerlein, E. *Föderalismus*. Bonn, 1972

Dicey, A.V. *Introduction to the Study of the Law of the Constitution*. Basingstoke, 1959 (1885)

Bibliography

Dienel, P. *Die Planungszelle.* Opladen, 1992

Duchacek, I.D. *Comparative Federalism,* New York 1970

Elkins, D. *Beyond Sovereignty: Territory and Political Economy in the Twenty-First Century.* Toronto, 1995

Erne, R., Gross, A., Kaufmann, B. and Kleger, H., eds. *Transnationale Demokratie.* Zürich, 1995

Eurobarometer, various issues

Eurobarometer, Top Decision-makers Survey – Summary Report 1996

European Constitutional Group, *A Constitutional Settlement,* London, 1993

European Parliament, Institutional Committee, *Second Report of the Institutional Committee on the Constitution of the European Union (Herman Report) of 9 February 1994*

Falkner, G. and Nentwich, M. *European Union: Democratic Perspectives after 1996.* Wien, 1995

Fishkin, J.S. *Democracy and Deliberation. New Directions for Democratic Reform.* New Haven and London, 1991

Fraenkel, E. *Deutschland und die westlichen Demokratien.* Stuttgart, 1964

Galbraith, J. *American Capitalism and the Concept of Countervailing Powers.* Boston, 1952

Germann, R.E. 'Bundesverfassung und "Europafähigkeit" der Schweiz', *Schweizerisches Jahrbuch für Politische Wissenschaft,* no. 30, 1990, pp. 17–28

Giddens, A. *Modernity and Self-Identity.* Oxford and Cambridge, 1991

Goodin, R.E. 'Designing Constitutions: The Political Constitution of a Mixed Commonwealth', *Political Studies,* vol. 44, 1996, pp. 635–46

Grande, E. 'Demokratische Legitimation und Europäische Integration', *Leviathan,* no. 3/96, 1996a, pp. 339–60

—— 'The State of Interest Groups in a Framework of Multi-Level Decision-Making: The Case of the European Union', *Journal of European Public Policy,* vol. 3, no. 3, 1996b, pp. 318–38

Grimm, D. *Braucht Europa eine Verfassung?.* München, 1994

Guéhenno, J.-M. *Das Ende der Demokratie.* Zürich, 1994

Guéna, Y. 'La Réforme de 1996 des Institutions de l'Union Européenne', *Les rapports du Sénat,* no. 224, tome 1&2. Paris, 1995

Habermas, J. *Strukturwandel der Öffentlichkeit.* Neuwied, 1962

Hedetoft, U. 'National Identities and European Integration 'from below'', *Revue d'integration/Journal of European Integration,* no. 1, 1994, pp. 1–28

Heinelt, H. ed., *Politiknetzwerke und europäische Strukturfondsförderung.* Opladen, 1996

Held, D. 'Democracy, the Nation-State and the Global System', in *Political Theory Today,* ed. D. Held. Cambridge and Oxford, 1991, pp. 197–235

Héritier, A., Mingers, S., Knill, C. and Becka, M. *Die Veränderung von Staatlichkeit in Europa.* Opladen, 1994

Hesse, J.J. and Wright, V., eds. *Federalising Europe?* Oxford, 1996

Hirschman, A.O. *Exit, Voice and Loyalty.* Cambridge (MA), 1970

Hirst, P. *Associative Democracy.* Cambridge and Oxford, 1994

Hobbes, T. *Leviathan.* 1651

Imboden, M. *Helvetisches Malaise.* Zürich, 1962

Inglehart, R. 'Public Opinion and Regional Integration', in *Regional Integration. Theory and Research,* eds. L.N. Lindberg and S.A. Scheingold. Cambridge (MA), 1971, pp. 160-91

Isensee, J. *Europa als politische Idee und rechtliche Form.* Berlin, 1994

Jachtenfuchs, M. 'Theoretical Perspectives on European Governance', *European Law Journal*, no. 2, 1995, pp. 115–33

Jachtenfuchs, M. and Kohler-Koch, B. 'Einleitung: Regieren in dynamischen Mehrebenensystemen', in *Europäische Integration*, eds. M. Jachtenfuchs and B. Kohler-Koch. Opladen, 1996, pp. 15–45

Jacobs, F., Corbett, R. and Shackleton, M. *The European Parliament*. London, 1995

Judge, D. *The Parliamentary State*. London, 1993

Kenis, P. and Schneider, V. 'Policy Networks and Policy Analysis', in *Policy Networks. Empirical Evidence and Theoretical Considerations*, eds. B. Marin and R. Mayntz. Frankfurt/Main, 1991, pp. 25–59

Kerremans, B. 'Do Institutions Make a Difference? Non-Institutionalism, Neo-Institutionalism, and the Logic of Common Decision-making in the European Union', *Governance*, vol. 9, no. 2, 1996, pp. 217–40

———' "Bon Courage" to the Third Level? Multi-Level Governance and the Belgian Subnational Involvement in the Council and the IGC from the Comparative Perspective', Paper presented at the ECPR Joint Session of Workshops, Workshop 21, Bern, 1997

Kielmansegg, P. 'Läßt sich die Europäische Union demokratisch verfassen?' *Europäische Rundschau*, no. 4, 1994, pp. 23–33

Kirchner, E.J. 'The European Community: A Transnational Democracy?', in *Developing Democracy*, eds. I. Budge and D. McKay. London, 1994, pp. 253–66

Koller, P. 'Theorien des Sozialkontrakts als Rechtfertigungsmodelle', in *Gerechtigkeit, Diskurs oder Macht?*, eds. L. Kern and H.P. Müller. Opladen, 1986, pp. 7–33

König, T. and Schulz, H. 'The Speed of European Union Legislative Decision making', Paper for the GAAC Young Scholars Workshop, University of Bremen, August 5–16, 1996

Landfried, C. *Bundesverfassungsgericht und Gesetzgeber*. Baden-Baden, 1984

Lane, J.-E. *Constitutions and Political Theory*. Manchester, 1996

Latham, E. *The Group Basis of Politics*. New York, 1965 (1952)

Laufer, H. and Fischer, T. *Föderalismus als Strukturprinzip für die Europäische Union*. Gütersloh, 1996

Lehmbruch, G. and Schmitter, P.C., eds. *Patterns of Corporatist Policy making*. London, 1982

Lepsius, M.R. 'Nationalstaat oder Nationalitätenstaat als Modell für die Weiterentwicklung der Europäischen Gemeinschaft', in *Staatswerdung Europas?* ed. R. Wildenmann. Baden-Baden, 1991, pp. 19–40

Lijphart, A. *Democracies. Patterns of Majoritarian and Consensus Government in Twenty-One Countries*. New Haven and London, 1984

Linder, W. *Swiss Democracy. Possible Solutions to Conflict in Multicultural Societies*. New York, 1994

Linder, W., Lanfranchi, P. and Weibel, E.R., eds. *Schweizer Eigenart – eigenartige Schweiz. Der Kleinstaat im Kräftefeld der europäischen Integration*. Bern, 1996

Locke, J. *Two Treatises of Government*. 1689

Luther, K.R. and Müller, W.C., eds. *Politics in Austria: Still a Case of Consociationalism*. London, 1992

Majone, G.; 'Independence versus Accountability?' *The European Yearbook of Comparative Government and Public Administration*, eds. J.J. Hesse and T.A.J. Toonen, vol. 1, 1994, pp. 117–40

Marin, B., ed. *Generalized Political Exchange. Antagonistic Cooperation and Integrated Policy Circuits*. Frankfurt/Main, 1990

Marks, G. 'Structural Policy in the European Community', in *Europolitics. Institutions and Policymaking in the "New" European Community*, ed. A.M. Sbragia. Washington DC, 1992, pp. 191–224

Marks, G., Scharpf, F.W., Schmitter, P.C. and Streeck, W. *Governance in the European Union*. London, 1996

Mazey, S. and Richardson, J., eds. *Lobbying in the European Community*. Oxford, 1993

———— 'EU Policy making: A Garbage Can or an Anticipatory and Consensual Policy Style?' in *Adjusting to Europe. The Impact of the European Union on National Institutions and Politics*, eds. Y. Mèny, P. Muller and J.-L. Quermonne. London and New York, 1996, pp. 41–58

Meehan, E. *Citizenship and the European Community*. London, 1993

Mény, Y., Muller, P. and Quermonne, J.-L., eds. *Adjusting to Europe. The Impact of the European Union on National Institutions and Politics*. London and New York, 1996

Mill, J.S. *Considerations on Representative Government*. 1861

Möckli, S. *Direkte Demokratie*. Bern, 1994

Mount, F. *The British Constitution Now. Recovery or Decline*. London, 1992

Müller-Brandeck-Bocquet, G. 'Ein föderalistisches Europa?', *Aus Politik und Zeitgeschichte*, no. 45/91, 1991, pp. 13–25

Neidhart, L. *Plebiszit und Pluralitäre Demokratie*. Bern, 1970

Nentwich, M. 'Opportunity Structures for Citizen's Participation: The Case of the European Union', in *Political Theory of Constitutional Choice*, eds. M. Nentwich and A. Weale. London, 1998 (forthcoming)

Noelle-Neumann, E. 'Die öffentliche Meinung', in *Jahrbuch der Europa-Integration 1991/1992*, eds. W. Weidenfeld and W. Wessels. Bonn, 1992, pp. 273–82

Norton, P. ed. *National Parliaments and the European Union*. London, 1996

Oates, W.E. *Fiscal Federalism*. New York, 1972

———— 'An Economist's Perspective on Fiscal Federalism' in *The Political Economy of Fiscal Federalism*, ed. W.E. Oates. Lexington (MA), 1977, pp. 3–30

Onestini, C. 'The Committee of the Regions: Origins of a New Supranational Organisation in Brussels', in *The European Yearbook of Comparative Government and Public Administration*, eds. J.J. Hesse and T.A.J. Toonen, vol. 1, 1994, pp. 163–84

Opp, K.-D. 'The Role of Voice in a Future Europe', *KYKLOS*, vol. 47, no 3, 1994, pp. 385–402

Philip Morris Institute, *Does Europe Need a Constitution?* Brussels, 1996, pp. 7-33

Putnam, R.D. 'Diplomacy and Domestic Politics: The Topic of Two-Level-Games', *International Organisation*, vol. 42, 1988, pp. 427–60

Rawls, J. *A Theory of Justice*. Cambridge (MA), 1971

Reflection Group, 'Report', in *Intergovernmental Conference (IGC '96)*, ed. General Secretariat of the Council of the European Union. Brussels, 1995, pp. 11–86

Reif, K. 'Das Demokratiedefizit der EG und die Chancen zu seiner Verringerung', *Politische Bildung*, no. 3, 1993, pp. 37-62

———— 'Public Opinion and European Integration – Long Term Trends: The General Pattern over the Past Decade', *Eurobarometer*, no. 43, Brussels, 1995, pp. ix–xxii

Rieger, E. 'The Common Agricultural Policy', in *Policy making in the European Union*, eds. H. Wallace and W. Wallace, 3rd edn. Oxford, 1996, pp. 97–123

Rosas, A. and Antola, E., eds. *A Citizens' Europe. In Search of a New Order*. London, 1995

Rousseau, J.J. *Le Contrat Social*. 1762

Scharpf, F.W. 'The Joint Decision Trap: Lessons from German Federalism and
European Integration', *Public Administration*, no. 3, 1988, pp. 239–78
—— ed. *Games in Hierarchies and Networks – Analytical and Empirical Approaches
to the Study of Governance Institutions*. Frankfurt/Main and New York, 1993a
—— 'Versuch über Demokratie im verhandelnden Staat', in *Verhandlungs-
demokratie, Interessenvermittlung, Regierbarkeit*, eds. R. Czada and M.G.
Schmidt. Opladen, 1993b, pp. 25–50
—— 'Community and Autonomy: Multilevel Policy-making in the European
Union', *Journal of European Public Policy*, vol. 1, no. 2, 1994a, pp. 219–42
—— *Optionen des Föderalismus in Deutschland und Europa*. Frankfurt/Main and
New York, 1994b
—— 'Negative and Positive Integration in the Political Economy of European
Welfare States', in *Governance in the European Union*, G. Marks, F.W. Scharpf,
P.C. Schmitter and W. Streeck. London, 1996, pp. 15–39
Schattschneider, E.E. *The Semisovereign People. A Realist's View of Democracy in
America*. New York, 1960
Schendelen, M.P.C.M. van, ed. *National Public and Private EC Lobbying*.
Aldershot, 1993
Schmalz-Bruns, R. *Reflexive Demokratie*. Baden-Baden, 1995
Schmitt, H. and Scheuer, A. 'Region – Nation – Europa', in *Das europäische
Mehrebenensystem*, eds. T. König, E. Rieger and H. Schmitt. Frankfurt/Main
and New York, 1996, pp. 164–79
Schmitter, P.C. 'Still the Century of Corporatism?' in *Trends Toward Corporatist
Intermediation*, eds. P.C. Schmitter and G. Lehmbruch. London and Beverly
Hills, 1979, pp. 7–52
—— 'Interests, Associations and Intermediation in Reformed Post-Liberal
Democracy', in *Staat und Verbände* (*Politische Vierteljahresschrift*, special issue,
no. 25), ed. W. Streeck. Opladen, 1994, pp. 160–71
—— 'Imagining the Future of the Euro-Polity with the Help of New Concepts' in
Governance in the European Union, G. Marks, F.W. Scharpf, P.C. Schmitter and
W. Streeck. London, 1996, pp. 121–65
Schneider, H. and Wessels, W., eds. *Föderale Union – Europas Zukunft?*. München
1994
Scholten, I. 'Corporatism and the Neo-Liberal Backlash in the Netherlands', in
Political Stability and Neo-Corporatism, ed. I. Scholten. London, 1987, pp. 120–52
Smith, J. *Voice of the People. The European Parliament in the 1990s*. London, 1995
Streeck, W. 'Politikverflechtung und Entscheidungslücke: Zum Verhältnis von
zwischenstaatlichen Beziehungen und sozialen Interessen im europäischen
Binnenmarkt', in *Die Reformfähigkeit von Industriegesellschaften*, eds. K.
Bentele, B. Reissert and R. Schettkat. Frankfurt/Main, 1995, pp. 101–28
Tsebelis, G. *Nested Games. Rational Choice in Comparative Politics*. Berkeley, 1990
Turner, J.H. *The Structure of Sociological Theory*. Belmont, 1991
Usher, J. *European Community Law and National Law. The Irreversible Transfer?*
London, 1981
Vibert, F. 'A Proposal for a European Constitution', in *The European Yearbook of
Comparative Government and Public Administration*, eds. J.J. Hesse and T.A.J.
Toonen, vol. 1. 1994, pp. 285–97
Wallace, H. 'The Institutions of the EU: Experience and Experiments', in *Policy-
making in the European Union*, eds. H. Wallace and W. Wallace, 3rd edn.
Oxford, 1996, pp. 37-68

Bibliography

Weale, A. 'Democratic Legitimacy and the Constitution of Europe', in *Democracy and Constitutional Culture in the Union of Europe*, eds. R. Bellamy et al. London, 1995, pp. 81-94

────── 'Between Representation and Constitutionalism in the European Union', in *Political Theory of Constitutional Choice*, eds. M. Nentwich and A. Weale. London, 1998 (forthcoming)

Weibel, E.R. and Feller, M. *Schweizerische Identität und Europa-Integration*. Bern, 1992

Weidenfeld, W., ed. *Wie Europa verfaßt sein soll – Materialien zur Politischen Union*. Gütersloh, 1991

────── *Reform der Europäischen Union. Materialien zur Revision des Maastrichter Vertrages 1996*. Gütersloh, 1995

Weiler, J.H.H., 'Der Staat über alles – Demos, Telos und die Maastricht-Entscheidung des Bundesverfassungsgerichts', *Jean Monnet WP*, no. 7, 1995

────── 'European Neo-Constitutionalism: In Search of Foundations for the European Constitutional Order', *Political Studies*, 44, 1996, pp. 517-33

Weiler, J.H.H. Haltern, U.R. and Mayer, F.C. 'European Democracy and its Critique', *West European Politics*, no. 3, 1995, pp. 4-39

Wessels, W. 'The Modern West European State and the European Union: Democratic Erosion or a New Kind of Polity?' in *The European Union: How Democratic is it?*, eds. S.S. Andersen and K.A. Eliassen. London, 1996, pp. 57-70

Westlake, M. *A Modern Guide to the European Parliament*, 2nd edn. London, 1995

Whelan, F.G. 'Prologue: Democratic Theory and the Boundary Problem' in *Liberal Democracy*, eds. R. Pennock and J.W. Chapman. New York, 1983, pp. 13-47

Williams, S. 'Sovereignty and Accountability in the European Community', *Political Quarterly*, vol. 61, 1990, pp. 299-317

Willke, H. *Entzauberung des Staates*. Königstein/Ts, 1983

Wolf, K.D. 'Defending State Autonomy: Intergovernmental Governance in the European Union', in *The Transformation of Governance in the European Union*, ed. B. Kohler-Koch. London, 1998 (forthcoming)

Zürn, M. 'Über den Staat und die Demokratie im europäischen Mehrebenensystem', *Politische Vierteljahresschrift*, vol. 37, no. 1, 1996, pp. 27-55

INDEX

Index

corporate actors 82, 101
corporatist system 5, 22, 144
Council (of the Ministers) 2, 4, 5, 21, 25, 27, 28, 30, 31, 36–42, 45, 46, 91, 95, 100–103, 122, 123, 125, 127, 128, 130, 131, 133, 134, 147, 154, 155, 161, 163, 164, 165
countervailing powers 69, 70, 76, 77, 84
creeping centralisation 50, 58
cross-national units 125
'Crucifix' affair 128, 129
CSU (Christlich Soziale Union) 39, 128, 129
cultural autonomy (s. cultural sovereignty)
cultural identity 72
cultural sovereignty 18, 127, 128

D
decentralisation 64, 65, 81, 108
decentralised unitary state 17
decision by non-decision 152, 153
decision-making costs 60, 99
decision-making pathologies 144 ff.
decision-making powers 9, 20–23, 36, 68, 92, 93, 103, 109
decision-making rules 8, 48, 58–62, 93, 94, 99, 163
deepening the Union 11, 163
default situation 60
deliberation 58, 87–89
deliberative opinion polls 89, 141
demarcation dispute 113
democracy *passim*
democracy-efficiency dilemma 141, 144, 147
democratic outlet 36, 103
democratisation 8, 9, 54 ff., 87, 91, 92, 95 ff., 160, 162
demos 32 ff., 54, 94, 96–98, 113, 126, 131, 135, 138, 139
Denmark 22, 33, 123, 130, 132, 133, 164
differentiation of competences 66
direct democracy 51, 102 ff., 139 ff., 155, 161, 162
direct-democratic veto 99, 103, 104, 109, 119, 121, 127, 135, 137, 138, 144, 146, 147, 149, 151, 153, 154, 159, 161
direct effect 2, 12, 21, 22, 54, 61, 96, 128
directive 1, 12, 14, 21, 129, 147, 153, 156
disarmament agreement 59
disembedding 75, 78, 138
disinterestedness 58, 141
divided sovereignty 17, 63
division of competences 2
Doppelmonarchie 3
double majorities 49
dual sovereignty 13, 49
dual structure 48, 49
Dublin summit 7, 163, 165
Dutch Social-Economic Council 41
dynamic of integration 157

E
Edinburgh agreement 45
educational policy 64, 128

effet utile 2
efficiency 143 ff.
electoral commission 116, 121
enumeration 67
environmental protection 106, 149, 152, 154, 168
Ermächtigungsgesetz 140
ethnos 33
Euro (currency) 7, 133, 163
Eurobarometer polls 32, 166
Europäische Sturkturkommission 46–48, 108
Europe of different speed 2, 164
Europe of the Regions 38, 40, 111
European Agricultural Guidance and Guarantee Fund 45
European citizen 32, 97, 119, 124–127, 163–167
European citizenship 33, 127
European Constitutional Group 26–29, 40, 41, 50, 67, 106, 109
European Court of Human Rights 14
European Court of Justice 1, 2, 5, 12, 14, 15, 17, 24, 33, 40, 43, 44, 95, 109, 121, 124, 131, 152, 155, 156
European Court of Review 12, 28
European Currency (s. Euro)
European Economic Area 140
European government 32
European identity 73, 85, 96, 101, 138, 148, 154
European majority 35, 101, 122, 126
European Monetary Institute 133
European Monetary Union 29, 133, 134, 163, 168
European Parliament 2, 4, 22, 26–28, 29 ff., 36, 41, 46, 47, 95, 98, 101, 119, 122, 125, 128, 130, 131, 133, 134, 155, 161, 164–167
European Parliamentarism 159
European parties (EPP, ESP) 34, 39, 101, 159
European Regional Development Fund 45
European Social Charter 14, 156
European social rights 33
European society 35, 92, 113
European Structural Funds 17, 47, 145
European Social Fund 45
European system of central banks 27
europeanisation 8, 34, 97
Europeanness 35, 105
Europol 164, 165
euro-politicians 5, 8, 11, 25, 125
Eurotopia 51, 118, 161
'ever closer Union' 11, 29, 128, 160
executive bias 24, 48
ex-post control 102
external effects 60, 113
exit and voice 57

F
federalist structures 16, 19, 24
federalism 16, 17, 19, 22, 24, 42 ff., 62 ff., 105 ff.

Index